AN AFRICAN AMERICAN EXPERIENCE

Volume III

A Socio-Cultural Examination of the African American as a Blues Experience

BLUES AESTHETIC IS THE PHILOSOPHICAL UNDER PINNING OF AFRICAN AMERICAN REPRESENTATION OF ART MUSIC DANCE AND THEATRE AS EXPRESSIONS OF BEAUTY

Delridge L. Hunter

Blues Aesthetics

Aesthetics: some personal thoughts

Brilliance
Originality
Par excellence
Extraordinary
Best performance
Best composition
Best arrangement
Best orchestration
Greatest improvisation
Lovable
Beautiful
Wonderful
Applause
Standing ovation
Bravo!

WHY HAVE JAZZ MUSICANS BEEN ASSSIGNED THE LEAST FAVORED POSITION WITH THE CULTURE INDUSTRY? WHY HAVE THE MUSICIANS WHO HAVE CREATED AND CONTINUE TO CREATE AN ORIGINAL MUSICAL FORM NOT RECEIVED THE RETURNS COMMENSERATE WITH THEIR CONTRIBUTION TO SOCIAL INTERCOURSE? WHY HAVE THE CREATIVE LABORERS WHO ARE THE INVENTORS OF DIVERSITY AND INCLUSION NOT BEEN OFFERED THE ACCLAIM USUALLY AWARDED TO SUCH ADVANCEMENTS?

Volume III has presented Blues as an Aesthetic musical art form that operates with a philosophical base rooted in the cultural forms that have developed over the centuries of African progression and transplanted to the United States during the Middle Passage.

It has examined the milieu of blues as the musical form that developed and grew within a process governed by its own rules of distinction. Its introduction from Africa permitted it to look at and reflect upon the socio-cultural infusions that developed as a result of interaction between the African, European, the Indigenous and other occupants.

Blues was important because every time there was a major social change, the music gave its own reflection of that change. Look at every period of socio-economic change within the polity of culture, and you will notice a new genre in blues has been invented. It is with this in mind that the reader may want to approach the conversation that goes on inside the discourse with defined, i.e., fine tooth, reading.

Table of Contents   **Pages**

Naming
Statement #1, Axiom 4
When a name identifies each member as an equal within the form, any additional name assigned to that member indicates that within the form the additional name is given a different value.

Statement #2, Axiom 4
Once the first form of distinction, e.g., "classical music", has been established and is accepted as the original and most favored position with a boundary surrounding it, a new form, e.g., blues, with a boundary is established as a separate form of distinction. The boundary of the new form establishes a position of inequality between forms.

Statement #3, Axiom 4
To create a form of distinction we must establish a boundary that separates the original as the first form of distinction from any other forms of distinction created thereafter. Once a boundary is established between these forms of distinction an inequality of value is assumed to exist between forms.

Statement #4, Axiom4
There must be a motive for one occupying the original position to offer names to other forms not considered part of the original form of distinction or of equal value thereof.

Statement #5, Axiom 4
Once the first form of distinction has been established and is accepted as the original and most favored position with a boundary surrounding it, a new form with a boundary is established as a separate form of distinction. The boundary of the new form establishes a position of inequality between forms.

Statement #6, Axiom 3
When a particular is considered the most favored, i.e., that particular is determined to occupy the most favored position of distinction. The name that particular assumes can be taken to indicate the value of the particular because of the position of distinction it occupies.

What is a Black Aesthetic?   23
Statement #7, Axiom 4
When a name identifies each member as an equal within the form, any additional name assigned to that member indicates that within the form the additional name assigns a different value to that name.

What is Black Popular Culture?   26
Statement #8, Axiom 2
To assign a particular process value greater than others, different names can be taken to indicate the value of each of the process assigned...To call a process by the name assigned indicates the value of the distinction assigned the process so named...Thus, to use that name to call this process again means the value is seen in the name called.

When does the Aesthetic Begin?   27

Statement #9, Axiom 3
It is through the usage of symbols called words that we call the name of each boundary created to separate one form of distinction from another. It is through the usage of words that a language is developed to give name to the form of distinction.

Black Music   29
What is its Relationship to Politics and/in Aesthetics
Statement #10, Axiom 10
When the name of a cultural activity is indicated to express the value of that particular process the form of distinction is indicated by the name. In other words, the name is an indication of the degree of value derived by and/or assigned to that form of distinction. Put differently, a particular culture thus indicated by an expression of the name is also an indication of the value assigned to that particular culture as a form of distinction.

Black Music: an Aesthetic Expression of BPC   30
What is it?
Statement #11, Axiom 1
Once a distinction is made for each particular as separate activity, one activity cannot reach the other formation without crossing the boundary that makes a distinction.

Black Music   31
How is the Creativity Expressed?
Statement #12, Axiom 2
When a particular group activity is considered the most favored as a creative expression, i.e., the group that performs that activity occupies the most favored position of distinction among groups, the name the most favored group assumes, can be taken to indicate the value of the activity because of the position of distinction it occupies.

Introduction

By its name, Black Music is to be used as a case in point. Because it is easy to identify, its contributions to popular culture are omnipresent. A good example of how this might be is in the performance of Black Creative Music (Jazz). Before we move further we must explain what we intend to examine when we use the term Black Creative Music.

In this discourse the words Black and White are applied as positions. As positions they represent all people from the least favored to the most favored in a given society. Color here applies as it may be used in playing the game of chess. In other words, it's reference to color, as description of people is not in use here. All people are subject to occupy many positions from the least favored to the most favored depending on the particular. Put differently do not mistaken black to mean "the color of ones skin." Here, black is used as a position as in chess.

Black Culture represents the cultural form that is identified as emanating within "popular culture." Popular culture contains the many forms that have represented what "common" people are said to invent, e.g., blues. Blues comes from the enslaved people who were brought to the United States from the continent of Africa. With them came a musical form that was performed with or without a vocalist, or, a vocalist without instrument. The music having its origin in Ethiopia, presents the Ethiopian, Harmonic Minor, and Pentatonic scales as the three traditional scales from Africa. These three are the basic tones of the many minor tones heard throughout the United States, Asia, and the African continent from Ethiopia through Mali to Congo/Angola. We call these scales the minor keys. As minor keys, how they are rendered, is determined by the presenter. The presenter is creator of the form and style of delivery. How the tones will be applied is left up to the lyric poet as a musician who has the desire to be heard delivering song by the means chosen by that composer. The philosophical form we apply to listening to the performance of this music   is   called   "Blues   Aesthetics."

Naming

Statement #1, Axiom 4
When a name identifies each member as an equal within the form, any additional name assigned to that member indicates that within the form the additional name assigns a different value to that name.

According to Kantian aesthetics, there is an assumption of equality, within the marketplace of art. There is a kind of purity that allows the artist and consumer to decide the aesthetic value of the piece of work under review. One may judge art on the merit of some assumptions agreed upon by the critical mass of an informed populace. However, within a polity of culture where the inequality principle operates, this does not appear to be the case: when one takes time to examine the marketplace of art of the consumer (inclusive), it becomes very apparent that art is not necessarily judged on merit. In this instance, we shall examine music as a way to see how an objective position of observation, whether visual or aural, allows aesthetics to inform the process; that is, the role aesthetics plays, if any, in permitting "good art" to receive appropriate recognition. The role of denial and non-recognition will serve as areas to review in our attempt to unravel art as a political tool in the process of recognition.

As a reference point, in our Law of Position, a position theory, "we take as given the idea of distinction and the idea of indication, and in order to make an indication we must first draw a distinction. We take therefore the form of distinction for the form. (Laws of Form, Spencer-Brown, 1) Thus, according to the Law of Position, a Position Theory, Axiom 4, the inequality principle is an operational form of distinction, i.e., a distinction is made between groups. A form of inequality is indicated by the name chosen to express the value assigned the particular form determined to be of less value. Once a value has been designated to that form by name, the name indicates the distinction in value attributed to the form so named. It goes further by stating, "There must be a motive for one occupying the original position to offer names to other forms not considered part of the original form of distinction…Once a name is chosen to indicate one form from another, motive has been established. The name assigned is supported by a definition and a value assigned to the name. A motive to distinguish one form from another by a name assigned a lesser value establishes an assumption of inequality between forms, e.g., fine Art vs. Folk Art (Axiom 4). Once a motive has been established the value assigned each form by the name called indicates that there is an assumed inequality between forms. In other words, all forms of equal distinction carry the same name. A different name assumes that there is difference of form. Thereby an unequal value attached to the name as a description of the form difference, establishes one called by that name as a position that is less favored than the most favored position. This describes a position of inequality of the Least Favored.

It is within the Basic Premise, Axioms 1, 2, 3 & 4, of Position Theory, that we shall examine the art called Blues as a form of Black Music and, as such, determine how it is governed by the rules of Blues Aesthetics. We shall examine the Blues form through its most artistic offspring, Jazz –so-called- in this discourse. Jazz or Black Creative Music (BCM) is chosen because it offers the best examples of how a particular polity of culture serves as the process that permits the most concrete manifestations of the interplay between Black Popular Culture and the culture of whiteness.

Discovery
Statement # 2, Axiom 4
Once the first form of distinction, e.g., "classical music," has been established and is accepted as the original and most favored position with a boundary surrounding it, a new form with a boundary is established, e.g., blues, as a separate form of distinction. The boundary of the new form establishes a position of inequality between forms.

With the organization of slavery within the confines of the United States of America there was an ongoing struggle between the Least Favored and The Most Favored over how culture was to be prescribed. From its inception, attempts by representatives of the Most Favored

Position were made to consciously destroy all of the cultural forms of the slave people as the Least Favored people. This effort to destroy the African sensibilities was carried on so that all forms of cultural definitions would be lost. The Principle of Inequality served as the operational form of distinction that was indicated by The White Position. Referred to as the Most Favored Position, the White Position represents the culture of whiteness. The white dynamic allowed it to claim ownership of what it did not invent, created or discovered and established copyright simply by applying the mark of distinction rule that states, "we take as given the idea of distinction and the idea of indication, and in order to make an indication we must draw a distinction. We therefore take the form of distinction for the form."

There are two forms of distinction: the Least Favored Position vis-à-vis the Most Favored Position. The authority invested in those who assumed the original position, thereby becoming the Most Favored People, allowed them to decide who would occupy as their nemesis the Least Favored Position. The slave was assigned that position. [The Least Favored Position is Black as in chess.] There was no authority invested in the Least Favored Position except that which a slave was supposed to do, whatever that was. A slave's role was to obey the Master and his surrogates. This form of slavery was totalitarian where few areas of opportunity were available for use. However, despite that the Most Favored's total authority and power was applied to destroy everything cultural. Despite the effort, a form of Black Culture was brought to the United States that remains, and sustains itself until this day. As a unique form of Black Culture, Devil Songs existed as an original lyrical form until "discovered" by Paul Lawrence Dunbar, W.E.B. Du Bois, Hart Wand and W.C. Handy. Today we know these, Devil (Sorrow) Songs as a form of music called Blues.

Blues became the most definitive cultural manifestation of blacks' survival of a virtual onslaught from the culture of whiteness. As Frantz Fanon's Black Skin, White Masks discourse on the struggle over the race/color mulatto, i.e., Creole, syndrome demonstrates, dialogically overtime the black skin complex became "the" obsession for (of) the Most Favored. An obsession with keeping slavery as a means of production was complemented by a system of inequality forcefully enacted to assure that the African did not cause any more disturbance than before. Laws enacted made distinctions that were clearly indicated by the form as each position was assigned by name. The motive for establishing a clear distinction was to assure that the African's place was well laid out and it was understood by everybody that these were the slaves and by the nature of this design they would occupy the Least Favored Position in society. The Principle of Inequality became operational as the mark of distinction. This form of distinction was indicated by the name Negro.

Cultural Tyranny
Statement #3, Axiom 4
To create a form of distinction we must establish a boundary that separates the original as the first form of distinction from any other forms of distinction created thereafter. Once a boundary is established between these forms of distinction an inequality of value is assumed to exist between forms.

During slavery, ongoing efforts were made by the Most Favored to dehumanize the Least Favored people so that their effort to oppose slavery would not face direct opposition. The people most feared were those enslaved artists who went about the community as carriers of the word through song and those whose humanity called them to oppose this institution with their lives. Respectful people called both "abolitionists". However, the word "abolitionist" was assigned to the most favored position while the least favored were "black" abolitionists: not even within their own struggle for freedom could they assume authority of the position as "abolitionists" without the attachment of "black." Why? The Black was the Least Favored, referred to by the name Negro; Negro was the Portuguese use of a proper name for "black", it meant the same. Negroes were the Least Favored because they were thought black in complexion as the children of Ham and Cain" The "color" black became "the Black" as the occupier of the Least Favored Position. As a Position, now, Black transcended color: it would apply to any of those whose distinctions indicated inequality. It applied anywhere there were least favored and most favored people.

A Sinful Case of Bad Faith
Statement #4, Axiom 4
There must be a motive for one occupying the original position to offer names to other forms not considered part of the original form of distinction or of equal value thereof.

Back to the story: Bad Faith existed when the most favored knew something was morally and ethically wrong but initiated conscious efforts to commit that wrong in order to deny the least favored people an ability to advance from their position. During the process of slavery, to control the least favored, the most favored outlawed manifestations of the cultural forms within slave practices that appeared to be too dangerous to the practices of slavery: playing ones percussion instrument was dangerous therefore, it must be outlawed; speaking in ones original tongue was prohibited, with a whipping forthcoming for such use of vernacular; worshipping in ones ancestral forms were called Devil worship, primitive, superstitious; and organizing meetings, reciting poems or singing lyrics that criticized unmercifully the master or members of his family and class were punishable by death. Such cultural forms, parent language, or mode of worship following the sacred texts, were immediately attacked and banned. The most apparent example of how serious the oppression was that, in most slave communities within the southern region of United States of America, the drum was a forbidden instrument because of the pre-telegram communication services it offered to the Least Favored.

To show how bias can blind reason, it never dawned on the Most Favored that they could take the drum, or an idea thereof, and create a "telegram" service for everybody long before the "telegram" was invented. The bias of non-recognition served to negate any effort to use the services of the slave beyond the capacity originally assigned. No member of the Most Favored position believed that the African —who built the best houses in the South, who knew how to raise cotton, plant rice and grain, which had photographic memory of the plans to build Washington, D.C., and other inventions and discoveries— was a capable being. No acknowledgement or recognition of any possibility of intelligence was shown. Put differently, when a member of the Least Favored invented something valuable to human and societal development, this invention was the assumed property of the most favored in that they could actually claim it as their invention because "Can't no nigger invent nothing." It is interesting how little if anything is ever mentioned about how this type of bias may have slowed the development of the South in terms of capital investment in communication and cultural awareness.

White bias would not allow a regional communication network designed and operated by Africans. How interesting that such a development would be comparable to the first canal built by slaves from Angola living in the Mid-Hudson Valley, New York State, connecting the Round Out on the Hudson River in Kingston, NY with the Delaware River near, Port Jarvis, NY. A regional communication network might have increased commerce by providing immediate communication while leading to other commercial inventions by the least favored. No one ever thought about that because reason was placed aside when it came to slavery and culture. Extreme bias acted as a disincentive to progress in the very region that suffered from a lack of growth and development because it stifled creative ideas regarding social intercourse. The previous example is only one of many major errors committed by the exclusion of the participation of the least favored that resulted from the cultural bias of the most favored.

Ugly Language
An anti-aesthetic practice of the most favored

Statement #5, Axiom 4
Once the first form of distinction has been established and is accepted as the original and most favored position with a boundary surrounding it, a new form with a boundary is established as a separate form of distinction. The boundary of the new form establishes a position of inequality between forms.

The investment in the slave as human capital employed as labor, failed to materialize into an economic advantage for the south. Their obsession with "bodies, black bodies" is only one of many poor judgment calls made in the polity called southern culture. As it turns out, the political, religious, social and cultural opposition gendered to remove black culture from the arena of civilization served to keep the art form we are going to around the Big House, inadvertently and/or deliberately did not inform their masters about the "bad" things going on within the community. To tell about these things would cause the most favored to think less of these tattle-tales. What we find was these 'kept' strivers, in the slave communities, suffered from their own triple life: one life for the master, one for the slave and another for self. They wanted to receive as much fairness, called privilege, as that bestowed upon the members of the most favored, so they often lived a shadow life. What was a shadow life? That was, when a member of the least favored acted like a "wanna be," so they did what they must do to stay within the favor of the Master Class in the Big House. As their complement, they lived in the shadow of the Big House.

They were the tattle-tales, i.e., the slaves who operated within the buffer strata: that group of the affluent-poor who are "middle class" in orientation and house servants in position. The tattletale buffer strata slaves wanted to avoid trouble as much as they could. One-way was to tell Misses all about what was happening within the slave community without ever giving away the secrets. Playing the role as tattletale of the buffer strata was not always easy. This was how it worked: well, no one mentions the "Hoo Doo" Priest and "Devil" singers except in the language that allowed the master to assume he knew what he really did not know. What did his family not know? They did not know that Black Popular Culture in the form of Blues was being developed right there on their "plantation." Nor did they know that this music would become the base and blueprint of American popular culture and creative music. He knew nothing about the black culture in the society in which he ruled, so he has no idea that what was being invented and invested within the slave communities where he it made suffering a focal point.

It was within the suffering that these so-called "sorrow songs" materialized through the lyrics and music style of the Lyric Poet. In other words, although the tattletale buffer strata were "informing" Marse, actually hu (he or she) was in reality offering no real information. Trivia carried more notice than substance. Besides, trivia substituted for information was much more interesting because it made good storytelling. In common language, or in what proper people like to call vernacular language. On the plantation, they called it, "bull shitting, or, talking stuff." The house Negroes spent much of their time bull shitting the master and his family by talking stuff. And, it was funny to them. "They get a kick out of it." This subterfuge, i.e., talking stuff, permitted lyric poets as social commentators to spew anti-slavery commentary and get away with it. Talking stuff simply meant the storyteller got away by making the story so real that the listener being entertained became so engrossed in the tale the she or he lost track of what was fact or fiction. How? The Master, as the most favored, is told, "Dat nigga be singing dat Devil music and telling Hoo Doo stories, dems Devil Songs, Marse you don't wanna hear dem Devil Songs, Marse Hunna. Naw! You don' wanna hear no Devil Songs," as she walks away grinning from ear to ear.

This off-handed offering of information had the effect providing safety to the lyric poet: The term Devil music meant one thing to the least favored and a completely different thing to The most favored. The assumption of fornication being the only thing on the minds of the least favored gave the most favored a false sense of security. Never did they think that the slave, occupier of the least favored position, would do such things as enlist in the U.S. military to the tune of 180,000 soldiers in the Army and be willing to lose over 30,000 to 40,000 in the war of liberation, or be so crazy as to join that zealot John Brown to start the war for the liberation of the Least Favored people, the slave.

Never checking these outlawed stories out, the most favored were left to their own imagination to visualize how the least favored operated within the community thought to be beyond redemption: the most favored figured that this Devil Music was the cause of fornication and all other kinds of lewd sinful wicked ways that this music perpetuated among the slaves. Little did the master know this lewd music was part of a repertoire that included a satire of the "marse's" family every night, never thinking that what the slaves were laughing over, way into the evening, were the tales about the "Bucksry," i.e., "the white man" that they never called "white"? We must recall that most of the tattle-tales were treated as "ole Annie," a good Negress who knew her place within the culture of whiteness. Getting word that someone from the Big House was coming, the lyric poet would segue into a blues tune about who's doing it to "whose ole' lady" or telling the story in song about "this is my man to night." These songs were humorous improvisations invented right there on the spot to give the impression that the performer was singing the same songs he or she was singing when the master appeared on the scene.   In turn, the most favored created their own fiction about how slaves operated. Cartoons, newsprint articles, wanted posters, and common gossip were the source of lies, distortions, and misinformation against the slave communities.

Bad Faith was the operational principle throughout this antebellum period. The effort at negation of the fallout that resulted from the physical violence permitted against the slave for "making the Overseer angry" was, in its crime, a successful time for the Lyric Poets. The blues singers of Devil Songs, the only real processors and communicators of the culture of whiteness that practiced overt racism, were the most persistent social commentators by offering lyrics as a critique of the slave master. The Lyric Poet had the appropriately ideal milieu to create the forum worthy of these criticisms of the master class in song: Blues song. Paying close attention to the historical development of Blues, it should be no surprise that this music reaches world acclaim. To survive, this creative art form —that was loosely structured music with a definitive lyric structure, where the lyrist would sing the first line twice with a minor change in the rendition the second time around— avoided the onslaught of the culture of whiteness. It survived intact without the white middle class of the south participating in the process. Poor whites, however, did hear and begin to play what they heard coming from the Lyric Poets. The question is how could "Southern Culture" begin to evolve as a form while omitting its most creative contributors: the stolen people of Africa? How could that be?

To complete the story, as a continuation of bad faith, in spite of [the planter class'] efforts to hide these Devil Songs, designs were implemented to dispose of the Devil worship called "Hoo Doo" and its related forms, Devil songs and stories. These forms were recognized as barriers to establishing a permanent institution of slavery. Fortunately they were not always successful in their efforts. Blues music, so called in the future, operated underground, oftentimes right in the midst of the Big House, with its true form reserved to be heard only by the faithful, i.e., those who really wanted to hear the old traditional music as it now sounded in the slaves' community. Operating within a process of two opposing forces, my/this thesis says for there to be conflict, the least favored has to continue to practice the ways of life they are able to maintain, resistance or not, while the most favored continued to ban such artistic forms.

Moving the analysis forward, one form that came with the African survived despite constant bombardment. That form of distinction has been sustained intact: it is now referred to as Blues. Despite the strength of the opposing forces, Blues continued to exist and persist according to its own principles of cultural formation juxtaposed with a practice that actively opposed the institution of slavery through criticisms offered as commentary in the form of song, oftentimes with the accompaniment of an instrument. Devil's music—as it was referred to by the most favored— as a form of social and political commentary became the mainstay of African existence. What is important to recognize here is Blues retained the unique three minor tones throughout the entire history of this political struggle in the United States? Even when later generations would rename and rearrange its related musical forms to take the sting out of their sails, untouched Blues continue to serve as compilation of performance styles wedded to the community ways of New Africa.

Politics and Aesthetics
Statement #6, Axiom 3
When a particular is considered the most favored, i.e., that particular is determined to occupy the most favored position of distinction, the name this particular assumes can be taken to indicate the value of the particular because of the position of distinction it occupies.

As politics and aesthetics inform each other they established as their interplay two processes: 1) the polity of culture established and sustained the conditions that allowed Blues forms to blossom; and 2) the musical form served as a continuum in the aesthetic appreciation of black music as attested to by the perception of its aficionados across the globe. This process demonstrates how an instructor may apply an integrative approach to the research, teaching and the study of "aesthetics and culture." By creating a theme as a basis for the study of, e.g., Aesthetics and the Political Economy of Blues, as a primary form in the development of American culture, an instructor may teach a particular course in a holistic manner. Such a theme allows an instructor to include texts from music scores, film, sound tracks, economics, oral history, social history, cultural anthropology, African American literature, sociology, polity, geography, psychology and criticism, or any variation thereof, as source materials for the course. Having a working knowledge of all disciplines simultaneously allows an instructor to integrate or treat as interdisciplinary materials designed to enhance the course.

Black Aesthetic
What is it?
Statement # 7, Axiom 4
When a name identifies each member as an equal within the form, any additional name assigned to that member indicates that within the form the additional name assigns a different value to that name.

A Black Aesthetic is the intuitive philosophical recognition of what constitutes a work of art (inclusive) as invented under/within the realm of Black Popular Culture. Black Popular Culture is a process of social intercourse that allows its audience to critique the value of the art as a subjectively arrived at process. That art, in this case music, is by performance standards an emotive intellectual intuitively pleasing piece. Be it a love song or social commentary, taste and preference are invented by creative labor. As a work process, a work in progress called creative labor invents the moment that its participants will witness the product in the making. Creative workers as laborers involved in the invention, serve as witnesses to and participants in the creative process as the work unfolds. This as a happening operates through its own dynamic.

What makes the dynamic creative and fascinating, thereby of aesthetic merit? The aesthetic merit is derived from neither the aficionados nor the group performing the music quite knowing where the performers are going with the particular creative work, a work that allows any number of improvisational possibilities that defy explanation. Very much aware of their roles as performers, their observations (listening) and informed discussions (playing) permit the invention of the work to unfold on stage as a performance demonstration. This mode of performance is arranged and conducted to allow the group performing that piece to express its full value. The level of creativity reached in their performance determines what makes that performance aesthetically pleasing as listened to by their aficionados. For the work to be judged of aesthetic merit that work or performance must be considered to fit within their definition of a black performance art.

The basic rule of a Blues-based performance art is the three (3) minor tones, the base of all black originated music; whatever genre derives from this music is influenced by or operates according to the rules governing the process of black music performance. That recognition constitutes agreement about what is creative yet utilitarian. The creative labor that produces these blues inventions is shared with and among that audience or, as Jim Hall, guitarist and composer said about Jazz as art music, "It does not play down to the audience." As its most common element, the audience may be present anywhere a performance is taking place. Moving to the present, performances now appear in places formerly considered "off limits," as well as the old venues always thought to be the appropriate location for "that type of music."

Blues Aesthetics, a Polity of Culture: a Position Theory applies the rules of Black Aesthetics to examine how Blues survived and evolved into the only original musical art in the uniquely American culture. The author has spent the last two decades researching and writing about the one musical form to survive as a continuum in a polity of culture whereby the terror of slavery, and sharecropping, were the norm of the day. The continuum, Blues, transcended this terror as music in both time and location because, despite offerings to the contrary, Blues could not be an invention of the United States. There is no need for such a claim. There is no need because it came with the culture brought from Africa. Its archaic sound makes that case very evident. By the same token, Jazz as a creative black form, could not have been invented in any other place than United States and have retained the Blues element so apparent in Jazz's development and growth. The invention of Jazz by African Americans in the United States was by no means an accident that could just as easily been invented by some other ethnic group, e.g., Italians. This is a preposterous notion that deserves no response. To call Jazz an "imperfect art with a questionable aesthetic" as Ted Gioia, a music critic, did in his work on Jazz, is only repeating

James Harris, who said, `music [is] at best...an imperfect art.' Harris was an eighteenth century European philosopher that wrote on music as an aesthetic.

All black music emanates from Blues and sounds the many different ways it does because it is an invention by the Least Favored of the United States. That statement should be a moot issue, but there is always the temptation to search for ways to deny its black beginnings. Blues is obviously older and different than anything the Africans came in contact with in this country. Being older it is performed by norms other than those developed in Europe. In a kind of arrogance of authority, however, the claim was that Blues must conform to European standards of beauty or violate European tastes. Despite its violations of the old norms of tastes, that is, what constitutes "beauty and the sacred," the artistic forms of Jazz established its own definition of beauty.

Blues evolved as a world-class integrative popular art form that applied lyrics and original musical scores improvised as a performance art. It has developed its own cultural form that informs the rest of society of what changes are at play. This communication is as easy as the three (3) minor tones that inform the "world beat" heard throughout world popular culture today. What does the aesthetic process observe?

Black Popular Culture
What is it?
Statement #8, Axiom 2
To assign a particular process value greater than others, different names can be taken to indicate the value of each of the process assigned...To call a process by the name assigned indicates the value of the distinction assigned the process so named...Thus, to use that name to call this process again means the value is seen in the name called.

Black Popular Culture is a creative expression of the social intercourse that takes place as the Least Favored People, called the Black, struggle to create ways of defining themselves. It has a cultural dynamic that is always moving, flexible, fluid, and creatively changing. The culture of the slave as the Least Favored was reconstructed around a desire for freedom. Their aim was/is freedom, it was a preoccupation. Despite the Most Favored people's occupation with a desire to create a totalitarian boundary around the Least Favored people, the Least Favored brought us music, dance, theatre, rhyme, verse, letters, song, worship, inventions, applied science, and other meaningful and aesthetically pleasing forms of expression. As for the personalities who composed and orchestrated these new present cultural forms, it was an expression of an individual's conscious efforts to define one's self in a manner that struck a balance between self and community, i.e., a balance within the community in which one lived.

Black Popular Culture
When did the aesthetic process begin?
Statement #9, Axiom 3
It is through the usage of symbols called words that we call the name of each boundary created to separate one form of distinction from another. It is through the usage of words that a language is developed to give name to the form of distinction.

Black Popular Culture (BPC) or Blues began as Africans struggled to retain, sustain and maintain those cultural forms that kept them in touch with the motherland upon arrival on the shores of the Americas. Retaining as many of her elements as possible did this. Retention came about through new symbol development. It was through symbols developed through the application of music and lyric that allowed Black Popular Culture to establish the base of its continuum. By continuum here we mean a process is established that allows the culture to live and thrive as an entity unto itself while it informs the majority culture. These new symbol as expressed in music and language informed the development of "American" culture. Although the intent of the Most Favored was to redefine the entire tradition of the African Cultural Forms, thereby causing their entire negation as a people, the process of oppression that resulted was too imperfect to realize that goal. The intent to offer only those elements that suited the Most Favored interest was implemented with uneven results and corresponding success. This made the process intended to redefine the Least Favored totally, that is, to make them into a new being, an unsuccessful effort. With this thought in mind we will put forth the following analysis.

This process of development of Black Popular Culture began during slavery. At that time, the critical mass of enslaved Africans in the slave society allowed them to congregate as a community and practice their cultural forms. These constituent residents resided in such numbers that they were de facto communities that amounted to hundreds of people who interacted daily. It was within these communities that the music from Africa thrived. It was also revised and expanded, and exhibited a great deal of diversity. African hymns and secular music grew and expanded side by side until Christianity became a competing force with the traditional practices of worship and other forms of daily life.

As the slave—the Least Favored—practiced more aspects of the culture of whiteness more barriers were established to contradict practices thought to be in conflict with institutionalizing slavery. Religious practices were the first to be outlawed. With converts to Christianity, traditional forms of praise were overturned and replaced. Hymns from Africa became new arrangements known as "spirituals". Undergoing many revisions, spirituals became acceptable because they spoke of those things thought complementary to the Most Favored.

The Most Favored obviously did not hear lyrics sung away from the "Big House." When heard by the Most Favored, these songs fell out of favor. Many became know as "secular" music. A genre of "secular" music that fell out of favor with the teachings of Christianity was indicated by the name "Devil's Music." To the Most Favored all black music was "Devil's Music"; for the new converts to Christianity, the slave, these were "Devil Songs," called En-gung in Congo. The presenters of Devil Songs continued the tradition of offering social commentary about the local happenings of the day. I refer to these plantation community criers, who sang Devil Songs, as Lyric Poets. They are the primary creators of the black aesthetic or Black Aesthetics.

Black Creative Music
"Aesthetics [and/or in] Politics"
What is the relationship?
Statement #10, Axiom 2
When the name of a cultural activity is indicated to express the value of that particular process the form of distinction is indicated by the name. In other words, the name is an indication of the degree of value derived by and/or assigned to that form of distinction. Put differently, a particular cultural activity thus indicated by an expression of the name is also an indication of the value assigned to that particular cultural activity as a form of distinction.

Black Popular Culture by its name +operates within a Polity of Culture. A Polity of Culture functions within the realm of politics and aesthetics. We might say politics meets aesthetics on the creative playground of Black Popular Culture. This complementarity serves to create such things as Black Music in its numerous genres. It is through the creation of Black Music the interplay between Aesthetics and Politics is acted out within this Polity of Culture.
Black Creative Music
An Aesthetic Expression of BPC
What is it? (Secular)
Statement #11, Axiom 1
Once a distinction is made for each particular as separate activity, one activity cannot reach the other formation without crossing the boundary that makes the distinction.

Black music, as En-gung (Blues), is a musical form that came with the African from places like Congo/Angola, Mali, Senegambia, and other places from Angola across the continent to Ethiopia. Its origin is the peculiar three- (3) minor-tone sound that makes what we now call the "blue" note. It is this sound that serves as the grounding for all music secular and religious within the black idiom. It is referred to generically as Black Music, but commonly as Blues. Aesthetically, Black Music's appeal to its listener is based on a sound that is often rhythmically enticing, e.g., Marvin Gaye's songs, with its strong sensual overtones is called Soul Music or Rhythm & Blues. Aficionados call it "getting in the groove." Thus, aesthetically speaking, Black Music violates the

Kantian premise that implies music is 'purposive without purpose' because the purpose is to dance or to offer (entice) other means of self-expression. Dance becomes a meditative experience that frees the spirit. Here the improvisational stream of this Black Creative Music may appear to offer the listener a tune that seems to present a "final without an end." The ongoing beat permits the dancer to reach cathartic levels of performance that often give the appearance of lewdness. However, there is no contradiction between the Black Creative Music and Black Dance because each derives it creativity from the three minor tones that govern the performance of Black Music as performed by that particular ensemble. Black Music has been in struggle with the so-called mainstream, involving an effort to deny black music its rhythmic pulse and its free spirit to change. The Most Favored as Devil's Music identified this mode of performance. This all takes place while the music is receiving acceptance by the populace. To show acceptance, the populace names each new genre. All names defy the title Devil Music given to Black Music called Blues.
Black Music

How is the Creativity Expressed?
Statement #12, Axiom 2
When a particular group activity is considered the Most Favored as a creative expression, i.e., the group that performs that activity occupies the Most Favored position of distinction among groups, the name the Most Favored group assumes, can be taken to indicate the value of the activity because of the position of distinction the group occupies.

The artistic beauty, brilliance, genius of creative labor, originality, and/or, inventiveness with purposeful expressions are the instances when aesthetics come alive in our examination of Black Music in general and Black Creative Music (Jazz) in particular. Blues through its most important forms will serve as the basis of this examination. Blues will serve as the means to discover how aesthetics evolve from an oppressed people's art within a polity of culture. It is through its modern music, the offspring of Blues called Jazz or Improvisational Black Creative Music that we may follow the development of an aesthetic premise surrounding Black Creative Music. The assumption is that the position Black Creative Music has assumed as "world music" says there is an aesthetic governing its movement. Further, the premise is Black Creative Music did not assume this position without a struggle with the Most Favored of the first magnitude.

Black Creative Music
What is the particular? (Secular)

Statement #13, Basic Premise
We take as given the idea of distinction and the idea of indication and that in order to make an indication you must create a distinction. We take therefore the form of distinction for the form.

The particular is a struggle between the Least Favored who occupies the Black Position and the Most favored who occupy the White position within a polity of culture. The actor is the Lyric Poet. The form of distinction that creates this dialectic involves Black Music in its struggle against the attempted dominance of the culture of whiteness. During slavery this struggle was indicated by two genres: religious and secular. Here we deal with the secular realizing the there is no real distinction between the two when it comes to contemporary gospel. Further, there is no need to accept as given these pseudo distinctions because within "Improvisational" music all sense of genre is dismissed as nonexistent phantoms operating within the shallows of the dominant culture.

Black Creative Music
The Music of Improvisation
Statement #14, Axiom 2

When the name of a performance activity is indicated to express the creative value of the group that performs this activity the form of distinction is indicated by the name…In other words, the name is an indication of the degree of the value derived by and/or assigned to performance as a form of distinction.

Black Creative Music, often referred to as Jazz, is the music of improvisation and, often times, a creative melodic composition with a harmonic construct. One demonstrates one's creative nature by composing the music right there on the spot, "an original experience" according to Bobby Matherne, as the audience looks on in awe. Creativity may be enhanced by actually writing a composition or creating a new arrangement of another song then improvising in solo form, or competitive poly forms, that embrace such combinations as duets and/or trios, as the musicians' interpretation of that piece. The idea is to perform the music at a level where the audience recognizes the creative talent through the inventiveness of the performer. Many musicians do this by spontaneously making sounds that translate into colors harmonically arranged to create streams of thoughts expressed musically. These original thoughts an improvised composition at this level require great technical skills that come from constant practice and experimentation with scales, sound, texture, fluidity and other forms of musical distinction. Constant practice is the manner in which one integrates the musical ideas into the conscious psyche of performance. Creativity is derived from this psyche. Such a psyche is able to act as producer of such thoughts that are expressed in the form of music. When performed in the manner intended, the audience and the performers immediately feel the aesthetic value of the performance simultaneously and in complementarity.

The usual requirements for a performer to become really gifted with his or her performance are those elements that are difficult to describe objectively. These elements are retained within the recesses of the other conscious. The other conscious is a gift of creativity and originality in that it elevates the performance to other levels. Performance is everything in Black Creative Music. It is through one's performances that the aficionados become familiar with the works of a particular musician. We must recall here that the reason for this discussion is this creative invention referred to in the "vernacular" as Jazz was invented by the Least Favored people in society. As a matter of fact, all of Black Music came from The Least Favored people who are called black.

Thusly stated, "Black" is both a color and a position. Aesthetically speaking, as a color, it is the least liked, except in automobiles, dresses, suits, shoes and women's under- garments. As a social position, black is the Least Favored in any society that operates within a classification system, what others prefer to call a "class arrangement." Thus to have a music aesthetic developed by and from the works of the Least Favored people as an original cultural form in that society is a sufficient rationale for the Most Favored not to offer accolades to the Least Favored musicians. To advance that musical form to the level of high performance, whereby the actual gift of the presenter is omnipresent within that performance deserves recognition of high merit. Yet within the society in which this Improvisational music was invented a denial of its existence and non-recognition of its performers as artists of the first order is still a problematic that has to be addressed.

A type of music that it is clearly an art form that serves as the base of American music should receive accolades in the form of state support as do the European classical forms and the teaching of the Humanities, Sciences, Management and other social forms considered important to the operation of social intercourse. As it is, this is the contradiction faced by performers of the music who come from the Least Favored cultural form in the United States. It has often been difficult to overcome. Facing this contradiction as an American and black, in an open society that promotes white as the Most Favored color, the treatment can be difficult to phantom.

The notion of applying "color" literally to people's skin tone should seem too ludicrous to be taken seriously. However, such arbitrary definitions can exist when distinctions are made between people as indicated by "skin color." Skin color becomes a position. Positions are classified as unequal, according to the mark of distinction as indicated by the name and position that is assigned to that color. To add insult to injury, the makers of the cultural forms that are adopted in this society are literally made invisible in an attempt to marginalize their existence. To ignore one's birth parents in an effort to have them disappear is tantamount to destroying them through denial that operates as a form of non-recognition. "Nigger as far as I am concerned you do not exist in my mind. I do not see you, hear you, or in any way acknowledge your existence. So get over it. It is not my problem."

The point is, despite all that I have said regarding Black Creative Music, with a few exceptions, it is not supported with subsidy. On the other hand, in New York City music that has it origin in Europe receives millions of dollars in funds from federal, state, city, and private donations. If Black Creative Music were not of equal quality to other art forms as a performance and concert art that receive subsidy from the state and private donations, maybe an argument could be made for not offering public support for the music. However, the music is recognized as exhibiting its own unique quality as an art form of a creative nature. The polity of culture serves as the mechanism for awarding merit to those considered as having made significant contributions to the advancement of the arts to popular culture.

Some maintain that to subsidize art will make the potential artists lazy and mediocre. It's interesting that when it comes to science or technological advancements no arguments are raised within the United States about gifts to research universities, institutes, and the like. So there is an obvious double standard used within the polity of culture that maintains that when a product emanates from the Least Favored it deserves little or no support except that offered by the marketplace of listeners who prefer that particular style of music. What we find is, despite the neglect of Black Creative Music from its base, Blues, to most of its listeners, 'Jazz' music continues to evolve new genres in a very frequent and creative manner. Just when one thinks there can be no more, another genre arises as if from ashes like the Phoenix.

How is this possible when no other musical form the world over seems to be able to do this? It is the three minor tones that permit this advancement in Black Music. It is the milieu of the creators that establishes the pre-conditions and maintains the conditions that encourage Black Music creativity. Black Creative Music is where the most advancement has been made in terms of music transition and transformation. As it changes each new genre continues to be judged on the merit of performance. Aesthetically speaking Blues as a continuum continues to offer world culture a musical form that is unique, challenging, beautiful and intellectually stimulating with an offering of "good taste" to its aficionados.

Good taste implies a sense of feeling good about what one just heard presented by the musicians in their performance. Simply put, Blues aesthetic is a subjective approach to appreciation. Aesthetically speaking, one can only appreciate what one feels about the music. Without feeling Black Creative Music is tasteless. This means it is without substance, a creative product that can only be realized through the creative labor of the performing musicians. Thus when it is said, "there was no feeling in the music tonight," the implications are that the performers are unable to reach the essence of Black Creative Music because they show no emotive qualities in their characterization of the process. There is no expression because it is lost in lack of feeling in the characterization of the piece. This loss of feeling offers no emotive substance that allows aficionados to feel the presence of the night's performance. Thus, for the aficionados that performance left no aesthetic appeal although the music may have been well presented, i.e., with the proper technique and knowledge of the music.

Back to the existential question, does Black Creative Music have a governing aesthetic? Yes, it does, unequivocally. What is it? It is the same process that governs all aesthetically pleasing music. Then, what is the problematic? The Most Favored want to take the birth- right from the Least Favored: it means control the masters. The Most Favored derive the primary benefits while the musicians get what remains, if there are any remains. In essence, if the Most Favored cannot control the means of production, they want to control its distribution. Control over the distribution allows the Most Favored to censor what lyrics are not allowed. So, although the war to destroy Black Popular Culture was not won by the Most Favored, their ability to market distribution gave them control over who and when the music was to be played until the new technology gave the consumer the appearance of the ability to play that role. A serious disadvantage was realized by the makers of Black Music when they were juxtaposed with record producers whose venture capital allowed them to record the "master" of a small unknown musician, pay them a small fee to sign the contract, and keep the master as their own copyright. The control of the musician's master gives the producer total control over what the outcome of any recording made by music maker will be. The failure to be able to defend the record producer forces Black Creative

Musicians to depend more on live performance for their work to be heard and seen. However, it is these live concerts that often produce the best music from most of these performances. It is here that the aficionados are allowed test their aesthetic judgment about what is good and what is bad on a given day.

The Culture Industry
A Post Marxist Point of Departure
A Point of Departure
Statement # 15, Axiom 1
Once a distinction is made for each formation, groups on each side of the boundary, being distinct can be identified as different. There can be no distinction of groups without motive. There can be no motive unless these groups are thought to differ in value. The group that holds the Most Favored form of distinction is considered to hold the most value. The intent and/or desire of the Least Favored group are to cross the boundary into the position occupied by that group. The value assumed by the group wanting to cross indicates the greater value awarded to and assumed by the Most Favored group.

Although, Theodor Adorno was at Columbia University, right in the heart of Harlem, at the time when Be Bop was at its height, he never would have understood BPC in general and Be Bop in particular. However that is no reason to dismiss his concept of the culture industry. I therefore take the name as a point of departure. This brief analysis of the culture industry will focus on the Political Economy of Black Music rather than a critique of his thesis, which others have done quite meticulously.

The culture industry, according to the Theodor Adorno theory, is a process whereby art – in this case music – is made into a commercial industry that codifies music into a product that can be bought and sold within the market place. The process that unfolds is the commoditization of the Least Favored. Those co modified through creative labors assume the status of producers as a factory worker does an automobile or a bar of soap. It is now a commodity no more, no less, to be bought and sold to consumers whose tastes are thought to be individually arrived upon. The Least Favored must serve as the distributor and consumer simultaneously. It is now a commodity no more, no less. As such, one can go into a virtual store download the music onto a disc or MP3, iPod, iTunes or whatever the latest model of down loading is and purchase the product sight unseen. In this case, one does have the opportunity to hear the music one is downloading and purchase it simultaneously. This means popular music now sells at a pace that defies thought.

According to Adorno, it is the process of codification that allows one to distinguish "high art," in this case, Jazz, from "low art," Rhythm/rock and roll/Blues, or in the case of "high art," "classical" from "pop" music. It is here where the contradiction arises. Purely speaking, Jazz, i.e., Black Creative Music, requires the same level of musical training as classical music. However, the substance Jazz is arbitrarily declared a "pop art" form. It is supposed that there is no basis in substance for this difference in classification. Such thinking places Jazz, a Black Art, in a situation that as an art form, its worth is never recognized for its true value to the culture industry. Put more in terms of how it is intended, "What rhyme or reason would anyone want to claim that Jazz is not a "pop" art?" This is clearly a misnomer. Therefore, the false labeling or classification is subjective and without foundation. This falsity is a bias that places a great burden on aficionados of Jazz because with such a listing this artistic music receives neither the support from the Most Favored as high art – except unevenly in some locations- nor the promotion to sell as a pop art within the market place of popular culture. The false listing places Jazz within a neuter territory as an art form. Jazz, in effect, suffers a non-recognition status in that it is neither pop (rock) nor classical (European). The denial of Jazz as an equal to European art music in effect is an attempted negation of America's unwanted child. Despite this status, as a negation of the negation, Jazz continues to attract the most gifted and creative musicians to its performance stage while it continues to serve as the vanguard of a classic musical form yet produced by musicians any place else in the world.

Unlike the old classical music of Europe and Asia, it has not become fossilized as one might think of classical music. Plus, all of its respective genres remain alive and active as performance music. However, unlike rock music, it does not receive the gigantic promotions, distributions, and sales in the market place of commercial music; nor does it receive the state and private donations from the upper middle class, the American equivalent to the European bourgeoisie. As a "pop art" it does not receive the promotion, distribution and other means of financial support that is awarded pop musicians whom the record industry wants to promote and support in the market place. The rationale for this lack of support is that Black Creative Music does not bring in the billions of dollars that one can expect from popular music. The same analysis applies to "classical" music. Yet, it is thought to be uncouth for a city of any worth within the United States not to have a symphony orchestra that is supported by a collection of finances from the State and/or private donations.

There is a kind of oddity here. There is some a level of financial support for Jazz concerts in places like New York City when a member of the Most Favored feels that there should be some financing for free concerts for public audiences. However, this support is very limited and not necessarily consistent. Financial support does not translate into the financial rewards approaching the magnitude of that brought in by the classical or pop music. Again, when a member of the Most Favored decides to support Jazz, those musicians tend to command more money per performance than comparable or even better artists performing at an event that are sponsored by members of the Least Favored position. Even when it is acknowledged that the event sponsored by the Least Favored was better attended and the performance was more exciting than one sponsored by members of the Most Favored Position, there is little or no State funding offered to these sponsors. The position of the Most Favored offers them an advantage never realized by those less favored.

It is this process that makes Black art music into an underdeveloped and poorly recognized commercial industry of culture. It is supposed that this is how music as an industry participates in the commercialization of art as a product to be bought and sold on the open market. The rationale of such treatment is this culture industry is expected to respond according to the laws of supply and demand.

No high art responds to the laws of supply and demand except on the low end of commercial demand. However, there may be some individual artists who may on occasion have luck in the market place at a given time. It appears to be more luck than any real genius that is rewarded. This means that because of its nature and the real contribution Black Creative Music makes to those other music genres that are able to function in the market place, Jazz should be rewarded accordingly. On what basis does Jazz deserve more financial support and social recognition? On the basis that the contributions it makes to the development of new musical forms, ideas and innovative concepts that result from the experimentation that goes on in Jazz makes it qualify for greater support than is given to date.

The new sound equations that pop music benefits from should suggest to a learned society that with more support the society is better off aesthetically and culturally. These new sounds in turn are what allow pop artists to simplify what they hear into a marketable product the public can relate to. This in turn allows pop "artists" to reap financial riches in the market place. This same analysis applies to Blues. Blues acts as the base and originator of new forms of sound that causes other genres to hear things that may be applied to their music that becomes a hit. It may be the same song but done by a member of the Most Favored in a more assessable sound that allow the song to become a hit. If the Blues composer (inclusive) does not protect him or her self, that person may lose all rights to the material composed and sung prior to a record company finding someone else to record the tune for public consumption. On the other hand, a record company may reap millions or even billions of dollars off of one Jazz masterpiece, i.e., Kind of Blue by Miles Davis.

The down side is what amounts to plagiarism is encouraged and permitted on the part of the Most Favored. What makes this plagiarism so disheartening to the Least Favored people in the Americas in general and the United States in particular is how plagiarism promotes having the music's originality attributed to those who have no foundation to create the musical forms they take. What is further disheartening is how the music owners of the recording industry will tell an artist what he or she must call his or her genre. The best examples of this are Elvis Presley and Jimmie Hendricks. Both wanted to be thought of as Blues singers and musicians. However, the A&R producers insisted on listing both as Rock 'n Roll performers. Here the Law of Position is best applied because color is not the issue. Elvis was called "white" while Hendricks was called "Black". Yet, each was, at different times, forced to embrace a name neither felt expressed who they were and what type of music they performed. Each was placed in this position because both came from the Least Favored people in the American cultural forms. Presley came from "po' white trash" while Hendricks was of mixed Native and African American origins. Thus regardless of national classification each came from the Least Favored position in the United States, and both were treated accordingly: Neither had much to say over their future. Both died tragic deaths that made them immortals and their recordings classic fixtures that will keep their record companies receiving royalties into infinity.

Although Blues, called En-gung by the Mbuwun people of the Bndundu Province, Congo, is the only original art form to evolve within the confines of these United States, it is still classified as "low art" or, when one is being polite, "folk" art. By placing Blues in a category that never permits it to gain an advantage, even members from the Most Favored seldom receive the rewards one receives from performing pop music. The fact is Blues should never be placed out side of the forum of art that permits it to benefit from the musical force it offers to world culture. As the producer of world music, it suffers from a similar position of a cotton picker who produces the cotton, yet can show little reward for that production.

The bias perpetuated against the Least Favored in this society, permits the culture industry to realize massive gains without investing in the product it receives from that position. What we are saying here is the culture industry tends to reflect the biases inherent in the overall society. One would think that with a producer deriving a living from a performance art for public consumption, the consumers who benefit from this product would provide a means of equalizing the gains awarded to the producer. That said the culture industry changes nothing.

Me Thinks
Statement # 16, Axiom 2
It is through the usage of symbols called words that we establish language as a means of indication of the motive that brings about a form of distinction. It is through the usage of language that we establish how crossing a boundary of distinction is determined or when that crossing is permitted. It is the usage of language that the motive has as a basis of expression for a form of distinction that is made.

The word Jazz is a very aesthetically pleasing name. If the basis of its claim is in, "I want to make love to you baby." I think that the word tells the story of what the creative energy is in this music called Jazz. Jazz in its most pleasing quality reveals how easily one can move from a melodic sound that is presented in harmony, to a harmonic blend of voicing that makes the melody a collective sound. Jazz voicing makes the music sensually pleasing when it is presented in an orchestration. Supposedly, Jazz had its origin in original sin: "lewd fornication in the den of inequity, the Devil's Church, the place of sinful luster." As a complement to this Least Favored's space, the location of the beginning Jazz, the term, beatifies the position of love making as a continuum that never ends. One loses contact with the actual space-time when the music is at its finest. Jazz, whether referred to as African American, Classical or Black Creative, or Improvisational Music, is still a sensual construct of sound that relieves the tension of everyday experiences.

Bluntly stated, Jass is a name we do not need to be ashamed of because of its origin. Although, "I wanna jass (sex) you up" may have been sung with a lewd intent and with ill begotten thoughts, the thoughts were not ill-conceived feelings of rudeness. Thus, to call this creative music Jazz, i.e., after the lewd lyrics of some Lyric Poet called a Blues musician, who was black, do really these same people invent a complement to the music? Singing the song with the chorus mentioned above gave name to a new process. The new process was symbolized by one letter representing an elbow (J) design of a saxophone, the other (A) with legs bent and spread apart, ending with two letters (SS) with the shape of two snakes makes Jass the music of original improvisation, an aesthetic of Black Art. So the Lyric Poet called it what it was, Jass. The word made sense. However, it was through the creative innovation of other musicians that the word Jass became known as Jazz, thus giving it a different aesthetic ring with more flavors. This was

Black Music in its most risqué form and delivery. Only the low life or simple people were responsible for risqué displays. These people were from the Least Favored people in society. After all, all of Black Music comes from the Least Favored people. The name, Jazz, as a gift to a musical form was not intentional I assure you, but it applied to and was immediately accepted by the Least Favored as their name for this good music presented in a manner they had never heard before. Put differently, it is the name of the Least Favored who has created all of the new music that permeates world culture, let us allow their voices to be heard using a name they created and love to use so dearly.

Jazz (Black Creative Music) is really the product of Blues aesthetics operating within a polity of culture. Now it is recognized as the contributor to, as inventors of, world popular culture. Being so, that recognition appears more acceptable if the honorees are descendants of people from the Most Favored Position. Their contributions are offered as more accepting from a member of the Most Favored. When their cultural icons embrace this vernacular form of music called Jazz, the Least Favored music is now legitimate within their boundary of civilization as defined by the culture of whiteness.

With Black Creative Music emanating from the Least Favored position, i.e., Black people, there is an attempt of the Most Favored to apply the rules differently when it comes to recognizing the Black Arts. In the United States, the Black Arts are judged as not holding to same significance to world culture as any art form that has as its base the culture of whiteness. That judgment operates without merit because as far as world popular culture is concerned, the proof is in the putting. Black Music in general and Black Creative Music in particular are equal to all and second to none. It is currently the most popular musical form in world culture.

The assumption of the dominant culture is because the birth place of Black Creative Music, is suppose to be the rural South, it can never expect to receive the same statute as that of "classical" music brought from Europe to the United States, by the Most Favored. This assumption allows two processes to evolve for the Most Favored: taking control of the intellectual property from the Least Favored, as their own without proper compensation, then selling the products derived from this false property ownership in the market place, thus gaining the material and financial benefits from such "ownership" at the total expense of the Least Favored, the creators of the product. By maintaining such "ownership," the propaganda of the Most Favored can sustain a constant perception of Black Creative Music is of less value because it comes from the Least Favored Position. The Least Favored Position negates any idea that Black Creative Music or the Black Arts in general can ever offer any value comparable to that retained for music identified as coming from the Most Favored Position. Despite the omnipresent effort to belittle cultural forms from the Least Favored Position, without subsidy Black Creative Music has attracted the most gifted musicians from across the globe to its performance stages. The attraction is its openness to innovation, change and other elements of creative energy that defy definition.

The intent of this discourse is to create conversation around a different way of looking at aesthetics and politics, aesthetics in politics, politics in aesthetics and political aesthetics. Within the discourse we employ A Position Theory as a mode and means of examination. By offering A Position Theory as a mode and means to examine social intercourse aesthetics is offered as a form of distinction that is indicated by the name Blues Aesthetics. Blues Aesthetics operates within a polity of culture.

Operating within the context of Black Creative Music, i.e., the Black Arts, Blues has evolved its own aesthetic principles of continuum. Within the continuum of Blues other Black Music development introduced a code of conduct regarding performance that evolved into a process that is infinite musically and lyrically. The code is expansive in that it allows levels of high performance for musicians so willing. Where no barriers beyond ones ability, perseverance, determination, and genius exist, gifted talent from the Least Favored Position find Blues forms willing configurations to compose within for any one so musically inclined.

The problematic is one must be willing to suffer the potential set backs that are always or at least oftentimes apparent for the people of the Least Favored Position who serve as the base of society. That position at the base allows others in more favored positions to misname, and therefore misrepresent, the base by offering it the name "bottom." "The bottom" is the lowest social ranking one can attain within the human intercourse called society.

However, to use the term as in the "Black Bottom Café" gives flavor to that name. To use Black Bottom, which is considered a racist/sexist representation of a Black Woman's behind, as the name of a Jazz Nite Spot, means that Jazz is played there. Does that not keep the stereotype about Black people alive? People at the bottom occupy the black position. Jazz is performed in a nightclub with a lewd name for a Black Woman that complements the type of music one should expect to hear by going there. Is that a negation of the negation? Or, is it an extension of the negation?

In the United States the position black represents every "color' "race" "ethnic group" including religious practices that occupy the Least Favored people in this society. However, the group that owns the official definition of the position called Black is people who claim African ancestry. Their "color", meaning skin tone, makes them simultaneously black in color and position. The position has its basis in the legal institution of slavery. American slaves were the "have-nots" or the untouchables, called the black, within this social context. Using the term "the Bottom" to advertise that this place is a Jazz Club seems to give the music that part of the aesthetic that creates the mystique so much apart of Jazz today, part fiction, part myth and part fact. Do we want to keep that alive as part of the Black Aesthetic?

It was the black that created the original music of the New World Colony called the United States. The music, Black Creative Music, often referred to as Jazz, offers an aesthetic system that has quickly become the artistic mode for creative musicians interested in expansive and experimental forms. Blues form is the most expansive music discovered to date. The three minor tones permit any equation to formulate within the genius of the music maker. With that knowledge it is no accident that these three tones serve as the root music for blues, spirituals, gospel, jazz, ragtime, stride, boogie woogie, swing, bebop, Afro-Cuban Jazz, cool, rhythm/rock 'n roll/blues, soul, disco, reggae, Afro Pop, and hip hop. Avant-garde, free form, experimental, ragtime and third stream integrated African-European musical forms into a performance mode uniquely black.

The ability to adapt to the culture of whiteness without ever loosing its essence is what made Blues Black Music. Blues simultaneously has become the original and only American form of music performed to survive in to-to by African people in the United States. This music was performed during the growth and development of American Civilization. It was the country background in places like Alabama, Arkansas, Georgia, Louisiana, Mississippi, the Carolinas, Tennessee and Texas that permitted Blues to survive in tact through compositions by unknown Lyric Poets and the likes of a Paul Laurence Dunbar, Bessie Smith, Memphis Minnie, Ma' Rainey, Sterling Brown and Langston Hughes.

Style and Aesthetics
Jazz is a form that allows the performer to apply the techniques of improvisation. Improvisation by its nature is an original happening that may appear as a spontaneously arrived at presentation. It does this by offering a performance governed by the blues aesthetic rules of style. Style is a mode of expression that allows a musician or musicians to distinguish themselves as performers of art music. Styles allow musicians to establish their unique ways of playing or vocalizing their presentations as an art form done as performance. Style permits a musician to "say what he or she says as creatively as the moment allows." Style is how the musician's ideas form a sound that an aficionado judges to be presented in a manner, which is unique. In short, style as a way of presenting music artistically. The aesthetic appreciation results when the uniqueness of the performance offers the audience a feeling of being there when it all happened.

After Thought
The Applause
Statement #17, Axiom 3
When the name of the group is indicated to express the value of the group the form of distinction is indicated by the name. In other words, the name is an indication of the degree of value derived by and/or assigned to that form of distinction.

Nothing is more revealing about a musician's performance than when one hears the name called is complemented with a loud applause followed by a standing ovation right after that's musician's ensemble has just completed a magnificent performance. The applause makes the performer feel ecstatic with delight. Nothing can be of more worth than the feel of recognition. This acknowledgement encourages the performer to compose more original works that appear to be pleasing to the audience's ear.

So the question remains,

WHY HAVE JAZZ MUSICANS BEEN ASSSIGNED THE LEAST FAVORED POSITION WITH THE CULTURE INDUSTRY? WHY HAVE THE MUSICIANS WHO HAVE CREATED AND CONTINUE TO CREATE AN ORIGINAL MUSICAL FORM NOT RECEIVED THE RETURNS COMMENSERATE WITH THEIR CONTRIBUTION TO SOCIAL INTERCOURSE? WHY HAVE THE CREATIVE LABORERS WHO ARE THE INVENTORS OF DIVERSITY NOT BEEEN OFFERED THE ACCLAIM USUALLY AWARDED TO SUCH ADVANCEMENTS?

Appendix

<<<A Continuum>>>
Law of Position, a Position Theory

Abstract

The Law of Position, a Position Theory, uses the premise of the Laws of Form as the basis of the numerous axioms that make up this paradigm. Each axiom contains a set of theorems that explain the rules of crossing, calling ((naming) and location (position) as operational forms within a polity of culture. Each axiom is layered to complement and support the others with axioms containing the rules that define distinction as an operational form of inequality. The two, operational processes here that explain the system are crossing and calling (naming).The position theory as a location theory, applies crossing and calling as indicators of the distance between the least favored and the most favored positions. The form of distinction as the original form establishes the motive for the creation of operational barriers to keep the other forms of distinction from crossing. To indicate what forms are to be distinguished from the original form, a name is to be attached to each form to inform that particular, what value is assigned to that name called. The name called and called again establishes that name as an indication of what form of distinction it is.

A Time of Discovery
While employed as an Expediter, at the H. Singer Zone Center in Rockford, Illinois from 1966-1969 I was introduced to a new theoretical construct called "Position Theory." Position Theory, I was told, was never written down by the author, a well respected clinical social worker, but it was well known within his institution because he taught it to his graduate students. After learning how he applied the new construct, I found the name useful in understanding other definitions of social arrangements. It may be applicable to almost every thing constructed.

Position Theory immediately resolved the problematic with theoretical constructs based on race/color/class, nationality/religion/creed, and gender/gender relations. As I now understand the theoretical frame, Position Theory applies to anything that has itself as its own particular while operating as part of a whole. Position with its broad and deep connotations in usage is a simple equation that can operate on any level or with anything, i.e., it can apply to any form of distinction.

In listening to my informants it was immediately revealed how Position Theory may inform my effort to understand the competition in complementarities of an open society by adapting it to the study of social intercourse. Position Theory [location] as applied here is an integrated process that involves applying many fields of study or disciplines simultaneously as one.   Prior to the development of integrative study more often than not research and instruction involved an examination of a piece of things or activities that happened in particular past, or after the fact, as a disciplinary, i.e., taken from the whole, a part/piece of) research or instructional procedure. No other ways of researching social forms was deemed legitimate: this is empiricism. This means of conducting research and instruction dominated university research for most of the 20th century. As we approach the first decade of the new millennium, the 21st century, the notion of disciplinary learning is no longer considered the only way of receiving a more focused understanding of behavior as it operates within the realm of social intercourse. [1996, C.E.]

The old process of dividing social intercourse into minute parts of study is now informed by integrating the focal points of complementary fields of inquiry. Offering a holistic view of any matter under discussion now complements disciplinary learning. Study in the realm of social intercourse that has developed within the polity of culture offers scholars a new way to examine the interaction between all of the other positions that exist as what I call the least and most favored positions in an open society.

A new paradigm is what the Position Theory has brought to the discussion on social constructs. It was in hearing the name Position Theory that allowed me to move beyond the old theoretical constructs I found wanting. The name position/location applies to anything and anybody, individual, group or any larger configuration thinkable that can be identified by calling the name. Creatively the Position Theory is like Blues, in that, it uses two processes: crossing and calling (naming and re-calling) to serve as the base of any observation made. Blues, the music of (from) Africa, allows any equation as a composition to be rendered simply by starting with three minor tones. Back during the late eighteenth and early nineteenth centuries, one could hear these minor tones played in Blues or any of the forms created out of that form of music.

With Blues serving as the analogy, here is a brief viewing of Position Theory as a working paradigm reflecting the manners or ways and means of Blues Aesthetics.

Position Theory maintains that to use crossing and calling as viable constructs permits scholars to inform their observations by realizing that crossing is a process operational when boundaries have been set and barriers erected. Either one crosses the barrier or one does not. A scholar may observe the activity-taking place as it is in motion during the movement to cross. An observation is made of the activity that is Omni-present and interactive. It allows one to study the position and the process.

Since the process of crossing is ongoing during this attempt to cross over, to learn the value of the crossing of one attempting to get over to the other side, one must know the name with a value attached to the crossing. As the challenge to the person seeking mobility, the crossing must possess a value equal to or greater than the name of the caller. Calling the name of the crossing, i.e., to go over to the other side, that has been named, gives value to the name called. It also shows the greater value assigned to the barrier erected to deny the crossing. The observations of crossing and calling are dynamic processes to be studied.

Social beings are always making adjustments with the knowledge that each has about movements in relationship to the information available about how and when to cross, if crossing is permissible. Crossing and calling have to do with the original mark of distinction made and barriers established by the entity that created the boundary. How a distinction is made and how the boundary is indicated to show a distinction is the role of language. The language that expresses the movement of entropy is what Position Theory allows one to investigate.

The likeness of Position Theory to Blues as a form of distinction is a demonstration of how the Position Theory may be used to inform scholars of what major contributions have been made directly by the least favored people. The information may be taken from the above statements regarding the minor tones. What has come out of the blues form of distinction is the invention of music the evolved into multiple sets that continued to expand. These new musical ideas all emanate from experiences working with three minor tones. The past creative activities are important contributions to the progression and development of world music. However, the contributions are virtually ignored by the dominant culture in the United States.

Applying the Position Theory, to the study of blues forms, allows scholars to see that the application of minor tones has resulted in the fundamental changes in modern music. This major contribution to music resulted from the creativity of the least favored people in society. Yet this music is not exemplified, as having any worth because the form of distinction casts on the contributors is that of the least favored position. Correspondingly, that same music adapted by members of the most favored, i.e., George Gershwin, assume more currency simply because these contributors hold positions as members of the most favored in society. With the George Gershwin analogy, what crossing the boundary has shown is it was only when a member of the most favored found blues in the form of Jazz a musical construct that could inform his work that the music began to receive acknowledgement as an artistic form worthy of listening to, i.e., worthy of recognition. Prior to his intervention, any artistic form emanating from the least favored was denied any crossing, except as the primitive works of a buffoon.

New Thinking Has Emerged

The least favored and the most favored as positions, have allowed me to observe bias as an operational form within the United States and most other polities of culture. However, my design as constructed within the least favored and most favored positions only allowed an application of black and white positions taken from chess. In other words, my initial design outlined the black and white positions as least favored and most favored, but did not advance the notion into a new paradigm until crossing and calling were understood.

The desire was to create a new workable paradigm. There was a need for a new premise supported by axioms. The idea was to create sets in the form of axioms that would offer new ways of examining social intercourse. Now the task was to give new definitions and language to the process.

The design of the Position Theory is to allow scholars to delve into how bias serves as a motive to establish a boundary of distinction in an open society. Must there be a motive for bias to become the ideological form that promotes discrimination? Must there be the intent to harm a particular group for bias to operate? Must there be a motive for one group to name another group that already has a form of indication that it accepts as defining who it is? These are questions   pondered after reading chapter 1, Laws of Form. This is getting ahead of the story.

Moving to New York City in 1977 after spending a year in E. St. Louis, six years in Rockford, Illinois, and seven years in Ithaca, New York, I visited all of the bookstores I came across in Greenwich Village, until I happened upon a small intellectual bookstore located on Astor Place between Broadway and Lafayette. What attracted me to the store was the sight of men dressed in European cut suits standing with a book in their hands as they perused these works with great interest. At some point during my visits, I noticed, located on a shelf in the window of the bookstore was a new book entitled, Laws of Form. G. Spencer-Brown, a mathematician/philosopher who taught at Cambridge University, wrote it.

At first I simply stared through the window at the book every time I visited the bookstore and wondered, "Who would write a book on laws of form and call it logic?" I always concluded as I entered the store, "It looks very interesting." Yet, I never looked for it on the shelf for quite some time. Instead, I wandered through the works that I had wanted to examine. I did not want to get side tracked. Eventually, I went to the philosophy section to look for the work to no avail. Not finding it, I approached the person at the counter and said, "Good afternoon, excuse me. Under what section will I find Laws of Form by G. Spencer-Brown?"

I recalled a surprised look of disdain immediately expressed across his body. He said after a great pause, with the obvious disdain still present and never bothering to return the salutation, "Laws of Form can be found in philosophy or mathematics, we have it located in both categories because of the nature of the work," as he turned his body away from his customer. I responded, understanding the tone, the language, and the gesture, "I looked in the philosophy section and it was not there, that is why I came to you, to seek your assistance." He was embarrassed. His bad behavior was so obvious that other customers looked on in amazement as they looked at me to see my response. I smiled at his behavior, shook my head in disbelief, as I walked away from the counter.

I discovered the book in the mathematics section, and did what was custom, tore the cellophane cover away from the brand new book and began to read it. I discovered unlike the other esoteric works there, it was in paperback. Not waiting to read the biographic sketch of the author and/or the review on the back of the book, I began reading the preface. I read it once. I read it again and again until I fully understood what was said. "That was only the preface," I said. "God Damn, this is some heavy doo doo." This is after my first reading. I thought, "Wow, this is interesting and I have not even read the introduction, yet. I could not get past the preface. I had never seen anything like this before. "I've got to buy this book." The price was around $20.00. The book became chapter one. That chapter became my obsession. It became the book. I would recite "We take as given the idea of distinction and the idea of indication, that in order to make an indication one must first make a distinction. We take therefore the form of distinction for the form." "Heavy! Heavy!"

As a catechism, I recited that chapter and verse everyday until rote memory took hold of the concept, the design, and the logic of the two constructs. The dual constructs called crossing and calling became my obsession. The two work in tandem. It is now understood that the notion of how crossing the boundary that is erected to keep someone out allows me to understand what the idea of crossing means under a new construct: the other variable necessary as a protector to crossing is calling. Everything must be called something. Everybody seems to require a name to be recognized by. The name is the indication of how a particular form will be recognized upon being called. What names will that particular person or group be called?

Papers, proceedings, articles, books, etc., on the Position Theory have been delivered at conferences and other gatherings of intellectuals. No matter the forum, it all comes back to chapter one. It is chapter one that retains my attention for the next twenty odd years until I finally get it.   All of the time spent pondering the Laws of Form my progress I share with my scholar learners in class. It is apparent that this sharing with my scholar learners over the school years has brought its rewards. The rewards come from having each class read the Laws of Form and the Position Theory and offer their own analyses of the constructs.

Writing the Law of Position

At last, in 2002, I sat down at a Barnes and Nobel bookstore in Poughkeepsie, NY and wrote what became four axioms. The premise plus axioms are what have emerged as a Law of Position, a position theory. A set of questions inform my Law of Position as an explanation of social intercourse as an operational form within the polity of the culture called the United States of America. My basic query is what form of distinction assumed the original and most favored position in the United States prior to it becoming a State.

Questions were developed in 1977-78 while conducting research for my Ph. D. thesis, The Puritan Invention, in Economics of Education, Education Policy Analysis and Africana Studies at Cornell University. My research led me to the Puritans. It was in studying the Puritans Invention that I thought of the idea of a most favored position as a working model for my thesis. [In 1978/79, I read the entire contract of the Massachusetts Bay Colony in old English at the New York Research Library on 5th Avenue and 42nd Street.]

As I read the contract, it becomes apparent that the most favored position is occupied by the European Americans, in the forms of Dutch, French and British, who have established themselves as occupiers of the original and therefore most favored position in the New World Colony to be called "America." Again, in complementarities the slaves from Africa by design will become the occupiers of the least favored position. As it were, the African American will occupy the least favored position while the European American will occupy the most favored position. The Indigenous Peoples who were virtually exterminated remained in the least favored as "insignificant" Historical Others whose Names were to be abused as (a)historical figures (objects).

The forms of indication that will give credence to those forms of distinction as the names they will retain and/or assign themselves as the original and most favored names, e.g., Winthrop and assign to others regarded as not of and less than As a starter, the European American renames himself "White Man" and assumes the name "America" to the United States of America. White now becomes a favored position expressed as a color of Homo sapiens from Europe. The name America will become the abbreviation of the United States of America. That will become the most favored color to represent the people who are superior. He renames the African Negro and all others accordingly. Black becomes the least favored position as a color to represent the people so defined, i. e., inferior. The white man is the "American" while all others are to affix another name to America to indicate that they too are Americans. From the inception of the New World Colony of North America, it has been "America" at the expense of the other Americas: North, Central, and South, Latino, French, British, Indigenous, Asian, and African.

Out of those two questions (p. 6), the Law of Position, a position theory, has evolved. The intent by the use of the first chapter of Spencer-Brown's work is to form the construct as my premise. The purpose is to investigate the forms of distinction and the forms of indication as they may apply within an open society, e.g. North America.

Introduction

The Law of Position, a Position Theory takes its form from the rules of chess regarding the black position vs. the white position. As applied within this context the black occupies the least favored position while the white occupies the most favored. Any appearance of likeness to past or current theories of chess, race/color/class, gender/sex, religion/creed, and other theories as forms of discourse is only coincidental. However, these previously mentioned theories are "positions" that may serve to inform the process of enquiry. One may say that the rules of distinction and indication apply to all of the previously mentioned theories.

How it works is by employing the Law of Position, a position theory, one may consciously apply the rules distinction and indication to any form that shows by name there is an indication of a mark of distinction without having to use the exception rule in the process. The exception rule is applied when those who are formally left out of the process are now included because they are thought of as exceptions: their skill level permits them entry. But, heretofore, they had no privy to enter, the new ability to enter, by a few made them exceptions. They become the Important Men always treated in History. Thus, although the Constitution of the Hau-de-no-sau-nee Confederacy was read with great interest by many of the Founding Fathers, no mention is made of this reading.

The Law of Position does not explicitly intend nor by implication attempt to negate the theories previously stated. Position as used here means a person is according the rules (ideas) of distinction and indication occupy a location or as a location a position. The positions according to these rules emanate from the most and least favored position as applied to chess.

However, in using the Law of Position, one does not have to apply the exception rule to a particular, when that particular fits within a discussion of a construct under any of the above systems of analyses.

A Basic Premise

We take as given the idea of distinction and the idea of indication, that in order to make an indication one must first make a distinction. We take therefore the form of distinction for the form. G. Spencer-Brown, 1979, Laws of Form, 1.

Axiom 1
The crossing indicates the distinction of the boundary.

By drawing a boundary between each group as separate formations, one formation cannot reach the other formation without crossing the boundary that makes a distinction, i.e., when a boundary between groups is set up, one group cannot reach the other group without crossing the boundary that separates them.

Once a distinction is made for each formation, groups on each side of the boundary, being distinct can be identified as different.   There can be no distinction of groups without motive. There can be no motive unless these groups are thought to differ in value. The group that holds the most favored form of distinction is considered to hold the most value. The intent and/or desire of the least favored groups are to cross the boundary into the position occupied by that group. The value assumed by the group wanting to cross indicates the greater value awarded to and assumed by the most favored group.

The group that holds the least favored form of distinction is considered to hold the least value. The intent and/or desire of the most favored group are not to cross the boundary into the position occupied by that group. The value assumed by the group not wanting to cross indicates the lesser value assigned to and imposed on the least favored group. For the least favored group who desires to enter the position of the most favored and then re-enter their own position, it is like they never entered the position of the most favored, at all.

No one from a group outside of the formation of the most favored position is permitted to enter their formation without approval from or by the most favored.

Groups not allowed to enter the position of the most favored are forbidden to enter the space of the most favored position. Forms of distinction are thereby indicated by positions assigned each competing, corresponding and complimentary group outside of the most favored position. Simply put, each group outside of the most favored position occupies a less favored position.

The extreme opposite group to the most favored is assigned and assumed to occupy the least favored position by those more favored.

Axiom 2
Words create the language of indication to describe the form of distinction.

It is through the usage of symbols called words that we establish language as a means of indication of the motive that brings about a form of distinction. It is through the usage of symbols called words that we call the name of each boundary created to separate one form of distinction from another. It is through the usage of words that a language is developed to give name to that form of distinction. It is through the usage of language that we establish how crossing a boundary of distinction is determined or when that crossing is permitted. It is the usage of language that the motive has a basis of expression for a form of distinction that is made. It is through the further usage of language that a distinction made is an indication of motive.

Put differently, a group thus indicated by an expression of the name is also an indication of the value assigned to that group as a form of distinction.

Axiom 3
The distinction of the claim is indicated by the name.

When a particular group is considered the most favored, i.e., the group that occupies the most favored position of distinction among groups, the name the most favored group assumes, can be taken to indicate the value of the group because of the position of distinction it occupies. To assign a particular group value greater than others, different names can be taken to indicate the value of each of the groups so assigned. To call a group by the name assigned or assumed indicates the value of the distinction enjoyed the group so named. To use that name to call the group again means the value is seen in the name called. The value assigned establishes a distinction that is indicated by the name called. The intent of those who occupy the most favored position is to limit those allowed and/or forbidden to use their name because that name is an indication of their more favored position as a form of distinction. Equally, when the name of the group is indicated to express the value of the group the form of distinction is indicated by the name.

In other words, the name is an indication of the degree of value derived by and/or assigned to that form of distinction.

Axiom 4
Principle as an Operational Form Of Distinction
The Inequality Distinction is an Indication of a Form of Inequality

A reminder: We take as given the idea of distinction and the idea of indication and in order to make an indication we must first draw a distinction. We take therefore the form of distinction for the form.

We take as given that the original form of distinction is the first form. Any other form of distinction created after the original form that is not of or from the original form is unequal in value to the original form. We take therefore the original form of distinction as the form that occupies the most favored position with the most value attributed to that position.

Once the first form of distinction has been established and is accepted as the original and most favored position with a boundary surrounding it, a new form with a boundary is established as a separate form of distinction. The boundary of the new form establishes a position of inequality between forms.

What we are contending here is, to create a form of distinction we must establish a boundary that separates the original as the first form of distinction from any other forms of distinction created thereafter. Once a boundary is established between these forms of distinction an inequality of value is assumed to exist between forms.

For a distinction of inequality to be made between each form a name is given to each [form] as a means of indication as to which [form] holds what distinction that is of more or less value than others.   That is, for the original form of distinction to be considered different and of greater value because of its originality, for any other form, a name is assigned to indicate the value of that particular form. The value assigned to each form of distinction is indicated by the name chosen to distinguish that form from other forms. Once a value has been designated to each form by name, the name indicates the distinction in value attributed to that form so named. There must be a motive for one occupying the original position to offer names to other forms not considered part of the original form of distinction or of equal value thereof. Once a name is chosen to indicate one form is of greater value than another a motive has been established. A motive to distinguish one form from another by name establishes an assumption of inequality between forms. Once a motive has been established, value assigned each form by the name called indicates that there is an assumed inequality between forms. In other words, all forms of equal distinction carry the same name.

A difference of name assumes that there is difference of form. That difference of form the distinction is indicated by the name given that form. Stated differently, an unequal value is attached to the name as a description of the form whereby difference establishes one called by that name a position that is less favored. This is called a position of inequality, i.e., a less favored position. When a name identifies each member as an equal within the form, i. e., each member has the same access as a possibility. Any additional name assigned to any member indicates that within the form the additional name has a different value assigned.

When different value assigned to a name is of less value than a more favored name a less favored position is established. Here greater access serves as the means of receiving a chance to advance ones position: a lesser degree of access offer less chances or opportunities to advance from a lesser position. This lack of access establishes a dialogical process of denial and non-recognition.

The lesser form of distinction offers less advantage of opportunity to that so indicated. Put differently, those with the greater degree of access receive a greater chance to advance their position, while those with lesser degree of access receive less chance to advance their or out of their position. In an open system whereby fluidity is operational, it is the degree of openness practiced within process that allows fluidity to provide the Least Favored access beyond that offered through fair practices of Affirmative Action.

Where unequal beings of consciousness exist, an inequality of position within the theatre of social intercourse is indicated by the names assigned.

Axiom 5
The Rule of Negation

The Negation Rule is designed to disallow the least favored any advancement of its position. It is also to disallow any advancement out of that position. The rule is to deny the movement of the least favored into any more favorable position. It is to make the attempt at upward mobility ineffective if not invalid. The intent is to break the complementarities' of positions that enrage efforts to allow those who occupy the least favored position any desk=re to create growth and development toward re-inventing themselves as a means of up mobility. Put differently, it is this denial of movement out of the least favored position. Thus, the mark of distinction in this instance allows the negation rule to deny the least favored from crossing the barrier. The inability to cross the barrier allows the naming and the calling of the name to place stigmas on the ones so named, e.g., Negro, Gypsies (Roma People), American Indians (Indigenous People of the Americas). Ad infinite

Naming (Inclusive)
The African renames Negro is used as an example of a process of negation by assigning a mark of distinction might be located and named to indicate who/what might be identified as people in bondage .
This is a case of the process operating.
Invention of the Negro
The Process

1. People Trafficking
The process of the invention of the Negro began with the People Trafficking of Africans from particular locations that supplied the workers necessary to perform the types of labor required to develop the agriculture, industrial and trade economy at that particular phase of economic development. The man stealing took place within these villages because they housed the types of workers who were needed to perform specific labor tasks. The labor tasks required dictated the skills sought out by the slavers. To steal people arbitrarily or on a whim was too inefficient and costly. So time was spent locating the "tribe" that performed the labor required developing the agricultural, industrial or trade economy.

2. Transporting
The process of the invention of the Negro moved to the second stage with the transportation of the African to the newly named colonized Americas.

3. Processing – Naming
The process of the invention of the Negro moved to the third stage by processing the African as a Negro into the system of bondage with the old Generic name being replaced by a new name, Negro. As the Negro, the people of the old continent no longer have a place of origin that is clearly defined, i.e., there is no Negro Land.

4. Locating

The process of the invention of the Negro moved to the forth stage with location of the African as a Negro into a colonial place, e.g. New Amsterdam, and living – work space now about to be given the new "Christian" name as an indentured servant.

5. Renaming—A new name for the African person, so-called Negro, a Christian name is the slave's name
The process of the invention of the Negro moved to the fifth stage with the renaming— naming of the Negro as (s) he is given a Christian first name that is to be certified as the official name of that slave.

6. Indenturing (position servitude)
The process of the invention of the Negro moved to the sixth stage with process of servitude being offered as a permanent position of the worker. The name indicates the position the name implies.

7. Enslaving
The process of the invention of the Negro moved to the seventh stage with the name Negro meaning slave and the Christian name meaning that is how that particular slave it be identified.

8. Enforcing
The process of the invention of the Negro moved to the eighth stage within the boundary being that of a slave established as the holder of the least favored position by law, with the name Negro indicating the boundary that serves to distinguish itself from the others.

The American Indian Construct
The American Indian construct uses that name of a people not thought to have any advancement worthy of being called by their names because they have no civilization. Not knowing that not all people want to live the way they live, and where India is or who the Indians are the name are the only one the European explorers knew to call any people thought to be where they think they are. Later American is added to assure everyone just learning about these people that they are some-place-else. The new information informs everyone that they were located in the Americas not Asia as previously imagined. Never acknowledging that these European voyagers did not know where they were in space and time, they would never state that these people are given the wrong name. They are given names of another people thousands of miles away. The notion is that they are going to keep that name because like the use of the word Negro the name according to C.L.R. James, serves a "commercial" purpose. People from another place should not be disadvantaged by having to learn every name of every ethnic group called "a tribe". As with the name Indian, the name tribe comes from within the European names of what they are at a different point in socio-cultural development. Likening the Indigenous communities to an understanding of how they developed, these people are thought to be at the "primitive" state of development. Thus, treatment of these communities is thought to worthy of the disadvantages placed upon them. Oppression is thought to be commiserate what mark of distinction is applied this group, so named. They are the least favored in the land mass just assumed to be their own decided these rules created under the Doctrine of Discovery or what the Americans call a state's "Manifest Destiny" give the most favored the Privileges and Immunity take and do what they want. For, they are founding a "new world 5has become the America Delrina

.

Examples of other names with a Mark of Distinction that are Indicated by these names: tribe, woman, white, black, savage, nigger, fag, dike, Mexican, Spanish, Bi-polar, rifer, ad finite...

Axiom 6
The Privileges and Immunity Clause of the 14th Amendment

The U.S. Constitution states, "No State shall make or enforce any law which shall abridge the privileges or immunities of citizens of the United States." By de facto use of (inclusive) this clause of the 14th Amendment written to protect the civil rights of the African American and others has been diverted to offer privileges and immunities to the least favored population that are called " po' white trash, Irish, Spic" etc., under the race construct.

Axiom 7
Catalyst
Location/production/process
A Catalyst offers, supplies, provides, makes possible, the means, the channel, the vehicle, the method, the medium, the mechanism, the access, to crossing the barrier.

Axiom 8

The Fairness Principle [The Catalyst Construct}
An operational form called affirmative action of the three (3) clauses of the 14th Amendment of the U.S. Constitution.
Under the fairness principle in a system whereby all social intercourse is equal, goods and services are offered at a fair market value. In a market system, it is in games, e.g., baseball, basketball, etc., that fairness may be practiced in its most objective form. Outside of games, fairness assumes that all goods, services and other forms of social intercourse are available to each according to the value held within the market place of supply and demand. Thus, it is only in games that fairness expresses a measure of merit. In other practices of social intercourse, fairness is awarded according to what position one holds. It, therefore, serves as an operational process of inequality between positions. In so doing the social interaction of it supersedes the ability to establish a "level playing field." In current society, that is called Affirmative Action.

Affirmative Action serves as the ways and means of providing access by establishing a process that offers equal opportunity to the least favored under the fairness principle. The motive is to establish a "level playing field," i.e., offering the least favored access to those areas and materials formally denied. In an effort to establish a level playing field access is provided to the Least Favored in the arenas of employment, housing, entertainment, play, education, the arts, civic life, and other ways and means of conducting social intercourse. Affirmative Action becomes the mode and means of measuring quantitatively the actual success rate, i.e., rate of return, of fairness as a practice within a society that employs two forms of distinction: The most and least favored.

With forms of distinction serving as a way of separating those who are most favored from those who are the least favored, equal opportunity moves the least favored no further away from their original position than before. Except for a change in the social order of inequality sustained by bias, fairness cannot be realized applying Affirmative Action as at means to better access through equal opportunity to all citizens (inclusive) of a given jurisdiction.

Affirmative Action operating within the confines of positions of favor, only permits fairness with a definable demonstrated outcome (DDO), e.g., baseball score of 5 to 4, when the process is conducted as games (a play activity) based on quantitative measurements. As an analogy to civil life, measurement on a quantitative level, Affirmative Action offers no quantitative or qualitative changes to show for its effort. There is no objective change in who occupies the least favored. Despite no meaningful change realized by the least favored, opposition to that effort has led the opponents to allege a false premise called reverse discrimination. Reverse discrimination presupposes that those at the bottom of the social scale once given the opportunity to advance will help the neighbors too, so?

A use of reverse discrimination by the least favored becomes a negation of the negation: Only the most favored can engage in reverse discrimination. That is what we call Affirmative Action. Reverse discrimination by the least favored becomes a reversal of the illusive forward movement the least favored have made on their own. Reverse discrimination supposes the power relationship to authority is one whereby the least favored now has power equal to that held by the most favored. That certainly is not how things are.

What the opposition is bringing to light is the appearance of unity among the least favored. Unity is not reverse discrimination. No matter, unity of the least favored is challenged as cheating, a violation of Affirmative Action thus undemocratic, as showing favoritism to members within the group. On the other hand the most favored is expected to choose from within their ranks for upward movement. It is they who must provide open access as a process for Affirmative Action to increase the value of those less favored. Even so, providing access to those previously denied can never completely reverse the discrimination suffered by these groups, as the least favored.

Put differently, the least favored are not in a position to engage in a practice reserved for the most favored: that of allowing an unequal distinction to be made between equals under the law. In effect the socially based, politically enacted inequality practices are not disturbed without a transformation of the market system regardless of allegations to the contrary.

To camouflage denial emanating through bias practice, a process called purchasing power parity (PPP) is offered as a way for creating a virtually level play field. In reality the whole notion of creating a mathematical economic formula for calculating parity as virtual when there is no value change, only sustains the inequality principle between positions involving social intercourse. What PPP does is offer an explanation of the vast differences between the two positions that is in a language understandable to the most favored. [This fore stated narrative can be found in the book, "Culture of Whiteness VS Black Popular Culture: a Law of Position" Amazon Books]

After Thought
Calling and Crossing

What I found interesting in my examination of Laws of Form was how easy it was to label others as exhibiting some disability or disadvantage, e. g., hair or skin color, that allowed them to be grouped with others for discriminatory purposes of who appears to exhibit the same disability or disadvantage. A disability in this instance is something someone else defines as have a displeasing (disabling) appearance (inclusive) thus placing him or her as a disadvantaged. The disabling appearance as a form of distinction identified is indicated by the name called. By calling those so identified with that name is designed to express the intent of the label, e. g., Negro meaning, from Africa, occupier of the least favored position, i.e., the black position, as in chess.   Location as a Position allows calling one Negro, the Latin word for Black in English, to assume the name to be negative. The name makes the Negro, the person, undesirable, i. e., the negation rule.

The motive for creating such a label is to discriminate against the group so named. Calling the name of those thought deserving of this form of distinction is done so as to identify to the greater community how such groups should be recognized when their name is called.

The intent of calling a group that is less favored by a name that carries disparaging results is to establish a barrier of entrance to the group so named. On the other side of the equation is the response of members of the group disparaged is to violate the rule, by crossing, the barrier of exclusion. Please recall, in an open society there are always stated rules of entrance and rejection. To overcome rejection, these ways and means of entrance are learned. Thus when a member of group disparaged happens to find ways of crossing the barrier they apply the rules and when successful they enter the new position by the ways and means they learned.

At this point, if entrance sought is not approved of, but serve as no deterrence to the upward mobility, other barriers are erected or set into place to limit entrance to only those things identified as permissible by the more favored groups. Engaging in the search for further entrance additional ways and means are sought out and applied. There are those who succeed, e.g., Miles Davis and Madam Walker, while others have failed, e.g., African American lyricists who made one hit. In other words, the less favored must thus find other avenues of crossing barriers that constantly appear as the next barrier – called hurdle – to over come.

The intent of erecting further barriers is to never allow, i.e., deny, that member of the least favored to gain enough favors to become a member of the particular most favored group, e.g., as in the case of Princeton University denying Paul Robeson entrance although he graduated Valedictorian of his Princeton High School graduating class. He was admitted to Rutgers, the State University of New Jersey, also a land-grant college. As things happen the least favored university in regard to Princeton was the recipient of a product of the least favored who surpassed the standards necessary for admittance into European culture, yet was denied entrance by the most favored.

For upward mobility in an open society to be realized, there appears to be a design, e.g., entrance to and graduation from a prestigious institution, a desire to enter and availability. Without access, fairness and merit there is less likelihood for admittance to operate in favor of the least favored as a group, e.g., Nina Simone, was denied entrance the famous music conservatory in Philadelphia. Some members of the least favored positions are allowed to cross the barrier erected to deny entrance based on the admission standard of that group, e.g., Collin Powell and Condoleezza Rice.

In other words, those allowed to cross the barrier are declared "qualified" members from the least favored. Stated differently, the possibilities of the removal of barriers that appear before a member of the least favored are nil to minuscule thus allowing only a selected few entrance. Further, entrance may be temporary as many have discovered after they have returned to their old positions e.g., many Rhythm and Blues/Rock and Roll "stars" fell from fame after a brief stay in the music business. A return to the old position is like never entering the new position.

Permanence is only realized when the offspring of the former members of the least favored group are accepted as members by those whose acceptance is considered representing the authority of group entrance. With this in mind, many families of least favored parents devote a life time prep their children to leave their old position, enter a new more advanced position and make allowances so that their offspring will remain there or advance further. These parents are willing to pay the opportunity costs to see their children are invested in as human capital. Epoch discourages or at least minimizes any notions of fairness; access and equality of opportunity that moves those currently in the most favored positions into positions lower than one they currently occupy. Thus relative expansion with proper investments assures the scholar learner invested in will be able to move into a better way of life than that enjoyed by the family at the moment. That idea is only doable in an open society.

What this dialectic or dialogic represents is its contradictions inherent in an open society based on what is required for the most favored to maintain social control. Looking at the current dynamic, the social arrangement of this of the number of members allowed into new more favored positions is one way of keeping its membership current and fluid.

References I

Alinsky, Saul, Twelve (12) rules for Radicals.
Butler, Octavia E. 1979. Kindred. Boston: Bea0con.
Chase-Riboud, Baraba.1979. Sally Hemings. (A Novel). Chicago: Chicago Review Press 2009.

Cox, Oliver Cromwell, 1970 Caste, Class, and Race: A Study in Social Dynamics. New York: Monthly Review Press.

Craig, William James. (Editor) 1916. The Complete Works of William Shakespeare. (Arranged by Henry M. Piironen).

De Tocquevilie, Alexis..(Trans Henry Reeve). Democracy in America.
Du Bois, W.E.B. 1909. The Souls of Black Folk. New York: Dover Publications, Inc,
______________. 1896. The Suppression of the African Slave Trade to the United States 1638-1870. New York Longmans, Greek, and Co.

Dunbar-Ortiz, Roxanne. An Indigenous Peoples History of the United States. ReVisioning America History.

Engels, Fredrich. 1888. The Communist Manifesto [English edition, edited by Fredrich Engels]

Fanon, Franc [trans. Richard Philcox]. 1967. Black Skin White Masks. New York: Grove Press.

_______________________________________. 1963. The Wretched of the Earth. New York: Drove Press.

Fazal, Tanisha M. 2007. State Death: The Politics and Geography of Conquest, Occupation, and Annexation. Princeton: Princeton University Press.

Handsberry, Loraine. 1958. A Raison in three Sun. New York: Random House

Henry, Winston, 1973. Strategy for a Black Agenda. New York: International Publishers.

James, C.L.R. 1963. The Black Jacobins. Vintage Books.

Kwame, Nkrumah. Neo-Colonialism, the Last Stage of Imperialism. ISBN-13: 978-0717801404. ISBN-10: 0717801403

Lynch, Willie. The Willie Lynch Letter and the Making of a Slave.   [A Fiction]

Marx, Karl. Das Capital.

Machivelli, Niccolo. 1469-1527. 1982. The Prince. Dover Publications, Inc.

Myrdal Gunnar. 1944. An American Dilemma, Harper Books.

Northup. Solomon. 1854. Twelve Years A Slave. Auburn: Derby and Miller.

Orwell, George. 1945. Animal Farm. New York: Harcourt.

Orwell, George. 1949. 1964. New York: Harcourt.

Rodney, Walter, 1972 (2011. How Europe Underdeveloped Africa.
Baltimore: Black Classic Press

Silman, IM Jerry. 1998. The Complete Book of Chess Strategy:
Grandmaster Techniques from A to Z. Los Angeles: Siles Press.

Smith, Adam. 2015. An Inquiry into the Nature and Causes of the Wealth of Nations. Irvine, CA: Xist Publishing.
Sunzi.

Spencer-Brown, G., 1979. Laws of Form.

Stowe, Harriet Beecher. Uncle Tom's Cabin or Life Among The Lowly. A Public Domain Book.

Wagner, Sally. 2001. Roesch. Sisters in Spirit: Haudeenosaunee (Iroquois) Influence on Early American Feminists. Summertown, Inn: Native Voices.

Williams, Eric. 1844 (2015). Capitalism and Slavery. Philadelphia: The Great Library Collection.

Woodson, Carter Godwin. 2010. The Mis-Education of the Negro. Seven Treasures Publications.

References II

Adorno, Theodor, 1997, the Aesthetic Theory, Minneapolis, MN: University of Minnesota Press.

Adorno, Theodor, 1991, the Culture Industry, London: Routledge.

Baker, Barbara A. 2003. The Blues Aesthetic and the Making of American Identity in the Literature of the South. New York: Peter Lang. Modern American Literature. Volume 38.

Baraka, Amiri. "The `Blues Aesthetics' And the `Black Aesthetics': Aesthetics as the Continuing Political History of a Culture," Black Music Research Journal .
• Vol.11, No. 2, Autumn, 1991.

Born in Slavery: Slave Narratives from the Federal Writers Project, 1936-1937: Washington, D.C. Library of Congress.

Brown, Sterling A. "The Blues as Folk Poetry." .O' Maelly, Robert G . Ed. 1998. The Jazz Cadence of American Culture. New York: Columbia University Press.530-551.

Chilton. John. 1987. Sidney Bechet: The Wizard of Jazz. London: The Manchester Free Press.

Evans, Bill. " Improvisation in jazz." O' Maelly, Robert G . Ed. 1998. The Jazz Cadence of American Culture. New York: Columbia University Press. 269-270. 1998.

Foster, Hal, 1998, Editor's Introduction, the Anti-Aesthetic, New York: The New Press.

Harris, James, 1744. Treatise the Second: Discourse on Music, Painting and Poetry, London.

Hume , David.   An Enquiry Concerning Human Understanding.

Hunter, Delridge L., 1995, The Jazz Worker: A Time of Crisis, 1980-1994, Dissertation, Cincinnati, OH: The Union Institute and University.

_________________, 2001, The Lyric Poet: A Blues Continuum. Brooklyn, NY: Caribbean Diaspora Press.

_________________, 2003, The Invention of the Negro: A Polity of Culture, West Park, NY: TransArt INC. Publishing.

_________________, 2003, The Position Theory, West Park, NY: TransArt, Inc.

_________________. 2005, "Sorrow Songs," Florida International University, African New World Studies International Conference on the Encyclopedia of the African Diaspora, May, 2005. Held at Florida Memorial University, Miami, Florida

_________________, 2005,"Blues Aesthetics: A Polity of Culture" (A Position Theory), International Conference on Politics [AND/IN] Aesthetics 4-9 June 2005 - Thessaloniki, Greece & Veliko Turnovo,

Bulgaria School of English, Aristotle University of Thessaloniki, Greece Department of English and American Studies, University of Veliko Turnovo, Bulgaria.

Kant, Immanuel . 1790. Critique On Aesthetic Judgment (Part I). Electronic Text Center, University of Virginia Library

Kofsky, Frank. 1998. John Coltrane and the Revolution of the 1960's. New York: Pathfinder.

Matherne, Bobby, "Book Review: Laws of Form by G. Spencer-Brown", Julian Press, New York, 1972, A Reader's Journal---Journey into Understanding, Vol. 1, 1999, Good Mountain Press Online Literary Reviews.

Murrray, Albert. 1997. The Blue Devils of Nana: a Contemporary American Approach to Aesthetic Statement. New York:

____________. 2000. Stomping the Blues. NY: De Capo Press.

____________. Improvisation and the Creative Process." O' Maelly, Robert G . Ed. 1998. The Jazz Cadence of American Culture. New York: Columbia University Press.111-113. 1998.

 O' Maelly, Robert G . Ed. 1998. The Jazz Cadence of American Culture. New York: Columbia University Press.

Powell, Richard J., "Art History and Black Memory: Toward a 'Blues Aesthetic.'"
Robert G. O' Meally, Ed. The Jazz Cadence of American Culture. New York: Columbia University Press. 182-195. 1998.

Schuiller, Friedrich. 1794-5. On the Aesthetic Education of Man, in a series of letters. Translated by Elizabeth M. Wilkinson and L.A. Willoughby. Oxford: Oxford University Press, 1967.

Schuller, Gunther. 1986. Musing: the musical world of Gunther Schuller. Oxford: Oxford University Press.

Snead, James A. "Repetition as a Figure of Black Culture." Robert G. O' Meally, Ed. The Jazz Cadence of American Culture. New York: Columbia University Press. 62-81. 1998.

Spencer-Brown, George, 1977, Laws of Form. London: New York: E.P. Dutton.

Troubadour, 2009, Online Encyclopedia.

Wilson, Olly. "Black Music as an Art Form." Robert G. O' Meally, Ed. The Jazz Cadence of American Culture. New York: Columbia University Press. 82-101. 1998.

DISCOGRAPHY

Count Basie
From Wikipedia, the free encyclopedia

- Count Basie Sextet (1954, Clef)
- Count Basie and the Kansas City 7 (1962, Impulse!)
- Basie Swingin' Voices Singin' (1966, EMI)

- Loose Walk (with Roy Eldridge) (1972, Pablo)
- Basie Jam (1973, Pablo)
- The Bosses (with Big Joe Turner) (1973)
- For the First Time (1974, Pablo)
- Satch and Josh (with Oscar Peterson)
- Basie & Zoot (with Zoot Sims) (1975, Pablo)
- For the Second Time (1975, Pablo)
- Basie Jam 2 (1976, Pablo)
- Basie Jam 3 (1976, Pablo)
- Kansas City 5 (1977, Pablo)
- The Gifted Ones (with Dizzy Gillespie) (1977, Pablo)
- Basie Jam: Montreux '77 (live) (1977, Pablo)
- Satch and Josh...Again (with Oscar Peterson) (1977, Pablo)
- Night Rider (with Oscar Peterson) (1978, Pablo)
- Count Basie Meets Oscar Peterson – The Timekeepers (with Oscar Peterson) (1978, Pablo)
- Yessir, That's My Baby (with Oscar Peterson) (1978, Pablo)
- Kansas City 8: Get Together (1979, Pablo)
- Kansas City 7 (1980, Pablo)
- Kansas City 6 (1981, Pablo)
- Mostly Blues...and Some Others (1983, Pablo)

JOHN COLTRANE

Impulse!

1961:

- Africa/Brass
- The Complete 1961 Village Vanguard Recordings (1961) (4 discs)

1962:

- Ballads
- Coltrane
- Duke Ellington & John Coltrane

1963:

- John Coltrane and Johnny Hartman
- Impressions
- Live at Birdland
- Newport '63

1964:

- Crescent
- A Love Supreme (RIAA: Gold)

1965:

- Ascension
- First Meditations
- Gleanings
- Infinity
- The John Coltrane Quartet Plays
- Kulu Sé Mama
- Live at the Half Note: One Up, One Down
- Live in Seattle
- Living Space

- The Major Works of John Coltrane
- Meditations
- Om
- To the Beat of a Different Drum
- Transition
- Selflessness: Featuring My Favorite Things
- Sun Ship
- New Thing at Newport [Coltrane on one side, Archie Shepp on the other]
-

Count Basie

From Wikipedia, the free encyclopedia

- Count Basie Sextet (1954, Clef)
- Count Basie and the Kansas City 7 (1962, Impulse!)
- Basie Swingin' Voices Singin' (1966, EMI)
- Loose Walk (with Roy Eldridge) (1972, Pablo)
- Basie Jam (1973, Pablo)
- The Bosses (with Big Joe Turner) (1973)
- For the First Time (1974, Pablo)
- Satch and Josh (with Oscar Peterson)
- Basie & Zoot (with Zoot Sims) (1975, Pablo)
- For the Second Time (1975, Pablo)
- Basie Jam 2 (1976, Pablo)
- Basie Jam 3 (1976, Pablo)
- Kansas City 5 (1977, Pablo)
- The Gifted Ones (with Dizzy Gillespie) (1977, Pablo)
- Basie Jam: Montreux '77 (live) (1977, Pablo)
- Satch and Josh...Again (with Oscar Peterson) (1977, Pablo)
- Night Rider (with Oscar Peterson) (1978, Pablo)
- Count Basie Meets Oscar Peterson – The Timekeepers (with Oscar Peterson) (1978, Pablo)
- Yessir, That's My Baby (with Oscar Peterson) (1978, Pablo)
- Kansas City 8: Get Together (1979, Pablo)
- Kansas City 7 (1980, Pablo)
- Kansas City 6 (1981, Pablo)
- Mostly Blues...and Some Others (1983, Pablo)

MILES DAVIS

COLUMBIA RECORDS

'Round About Midnight
- Released: March 18, 1957
- Recorded: October 27, 1955 – June 5, 1956
- Label: Columbia
Format: LP

Miles Ahead
- Released: 1957
- Recorded: May 6, 1957 – August 22, 1957
- Label: Columbia
- Format: LP

Milestones
- Released: 1958
- Recorded: April 2, 1958 – April 3, 1958
- Label: Columbia
- Format: LP

Porgy and Bess
- Released: 1958
- Recorded: July 22, 1958 – August 18, 1958
- Label: Columbia
- Format: LP

1958 Miles
- Released: 1958
- Recorded: May 26, 1958
- Label: Columbia
- Format: LP

Kind of Blue
- Released: August 17, 1959
- Recorded: March 2, 1959 – April 22, 1959
- Label: Columbia
Format: LP, Reel Tape

Sketches of Spain
- Released: July 18, 1960
- Recorded: November 15, 1959 – November 20, 1959
- Label: Columbia
Format: LP, Reel Tape

Someday My Prince Will Come
- Released: December 11, 1961
- Recorded: March 7, 1961 – March 21, 1961
- Label: Columbia
Format: LP

Quiet Nights(with Gil Evans)
- Released: December 1963
- Recorded: July 27, 1962 – April 17, 1963
- Label: Columbia
Format: LP, Reel Tape

Quiet Nights(with Gil Evans)
- Released: December 1963
- Recorded: July 27, 1962 – April 17, 1963
- Label: Columbia
Format: LP, Reel Tape

Seven Steps to Heaven
- Released: 1963
- Recorded: April 16, 1963 – May 14, 1963
- Label: Columbia

- Format: LP, Reel Tape

E.S.P.
- Released: November 1965
- Recorded: January 20, 1965 – January 22, 1965
- Label: Columbia
Format: LP

Sorcerer
- Released: 1967
- Recorded: August 21, 1962 – May 24, 1967
- Label: Columbia
Format: LP

Nefertiti
- Released: 1968
- Recorded: June 7, 1967 – July 19, 1967
- Label: Columbia
Format: LP

Miles in the Sky
- Released: 1968
- Recorded: January 16, 1968 – May 17, 1968
- Label: Columbia
Format: LP

Filles de Kilimanjaro
- Released: January 29, 1969
- Recorded: June 19, 1968 – September 24, 1968
- Label: Columbia
Format: LP, Reel Tape

In a Silent Way
- Released: July 30, 1969
- Recorded: February 18, 1969
- Label: Columbia
Format: LP

Bitches Brew
- Released: April 1970
- Recorded: August 19, 1969 – January 28, 1970
- Label: Columbia
Format: LP, Reel Tape

A Tribute to Jack Johnson
- Released: February 24, 1971
- Recorded: February 18 – April 7, 1970
- Label: Columbia
- Format: LP, CD, CS

Live-Evil
- Released: November 17, 1971
- Recorded: February 6, 1970 – December 19, 1970

- Label: Columbia
Format: LP, CD

On the Corner
- Released: October 11, 1972
- Recorded: June 1, 1972 – June 6, 1972
- Label: Columbia
- Format: LP, CD

Big Fun
- Released: April 19, 1974
- Recorded: November 19, 1969 – June 12, 1972
- Label: Columbia
Format: LP, CD

Get Up with It
- Released: November 22, 1974
- Recorded: May 19, 1970 – October 7, 1974
- Label: Columbia
Format: CD

Water Babies
- Released: November 2, 1976
- Recorded: June 1967 – November 1968
- Label: Columbia
Format: CD

Kenny Dorham
(From Wikipedia, the free encyclopedia)

As leader

- 1953: Kenny Dorham Quintet (Debut)
- 1955: Afro-Cuban (Blue Note)
- 1956: 'Round About Midnight at the Cafe Bohemia (Blue Note)
- 1957: Jazz Contrasts (Riverside) featuring Sonny Rollins
- 1957: 2 Horns / 2 Rhythm (Riverside) featuring Ernie Henry
- 1958: This Is the Moment! (Riverside)
- 1959: Blue Spring (Riverside) with Cannonball Adderley
- 1959: Quiet Kenny (New Jazz)
- 1960: The Kenny Dorham Memorial Album (Xanadu)
- 1960: Jazz Contemporary (Time)
- 1960: Show Boat (Time)
- 1961: Whistle Stop (Blue Note)
- 1961: Inta Somethin' (Pacific Jazz)
- 1962: Matador (United Artists)
- 1963: Una Mas (Blue Note)
- 1963: Scandia Skies (SteepleChase)
- 1963: Short Story (SteepleChase)
- 1964: Trompeta Toccata (Blue Note)

Duke Ellington

(From Wikipedia, the free encyclopedia)

Compilations

- Complete Works: 1924-1947 (Proper UK) (2003) (40 discs)
- The Centennial Edition: The Complete RCA-Victor Recordings (1999) (24 discs)
- The Complete RCA-Victor Mid-Forties Recordings (2000)
- The Private Collection (1956–1971) (Saja) (10 discs)
- The Duke Box (Storyville) (2007) (8 discs)
- 1936-40 Small Group Sessions (Mosaic) (7 discs)
- The Complete Capitol Recordings (Blue Note) (1999) (5 discs)
- The Reprise Studio Recordings (Mosaic) (5 discs)
- Early Ellington: The Complete Brunswick And Vocalion Recordings Of
- Duke Ellington, 1926-1931 (GRP Records/ Verve Music Group) (3 discs)
- Masterpieces, 1926-1949 (Proper) (4 discs)
- The Gold Collection, 40 Classic Performances (Proper/Retro) (2 discs)
- Duke Ellington's Incidental Music for Shakespeare's Play Timon of Athens, adapted by Stanley Silverman (1993). Ellington does not perform on this recording, but it includes previously unreleased compositions.

Charlie Parker
1949

- Charlie Parker - Broadcast Performances, Vol. 2 (ESP)
- The Metronome All Stars - From Swing To Be-Bop (RCA Camden)
- Jazz At The Philharmonic - J.A.T.P. At Carnegie Hall 1949 (Pablo)
- Rara Avis Avis, Rare Bird (Stash)
- Various Artists - Alto Saxes (Norgran)
- Bird On The Road (Jazz Showcase)
- Charlie Parker/Dizzy Gillespie - Bird And Diz (Universal (Japan))
- Charlie Parker - Bird In Paris (Bird in Paris)
- Charlie Parker In France 1949 (Jazz O.P. (France))
- Charlie Parker - Bird Box, Vol. 2 (Jazz Up (Italy))
- Bird's Eyes, Vol. 5 (Philology)
- Charlie Parker with Strings (Clef)
- Bird's Eyes, Vol. 2 (Philology)
- Bird's Eyes, Vol. 3 (Philology)
- Dance Of The Infidels (S.C.A.M.)

www.ingramcontent.com/pod-product-compliance
Lightning Source LLC
Chambersburg PA
CBHW080817280726
48660CB00018B/3486